100 Years of Purses

1880s to 1980s

Identification
&
Values

Ronna Lee Aikins

COLLECTOR BOOKS
A Division of Schroeder Publishing Co., Inc.

Cover design by Beth Summers
Book design by Terri Hunter

COLLECTOR BOOKS
P.O. Box 3009
Paducah, Kentucky 42002-3009
www.collectorbooks.com

The current values in this book should be used only as a guide. They are not intended to set prices, which vary from one section of the country to another. Auction prices as well as dealer prices vary greatly and are affected by condition as well as demand. Neither the authors nor the publisher assumes responsibility for any losses that might be incurred as a result of consulting this guide.

Searching For A Publisher?

We are always looking for people knowledgeable within their fields.
If you feel that there is a real need for a book on your collectible subject
and have a large comprehensive collection, contact Collector Books.

Contents

Dedication

This book holds a special place in my heart. Katie, my daughter, has the love of collecting purses. She has an infatuation with purses that began when she was 16 months old. Today, Katie knows how to carry, purchase, use, and collect purses. She knows how to choose a purse to reflect her mood. Her purses and shoes are prized possessions.

It has been a great pleasure to shop with her for her beauties. She constantly amazes me with her finds and purchases from her treasure hunts.

Katie, I am so thrilled that you have a great collection that you can continue to add to. You may even wonder who once carried your purses, and to where, what was carried in the bags, and when and where they were first purchased. It is my hope that you view this book with passion. It is for you that I documented your collection. Always enjoy and share with your friends your love of purses.

Always remember our mother-daughter shopping trips and the purses that carried your mom's wallet so that she could purchase the bags. Shopping with you is always worth the purse and pleasure. Keep up the collection. I love you so.

Mom

Acknowledgments

Bob and Kathy Watson, thank you for sharing your vintage bags and your stories with me. It is always fun to see Kathy's finds. Keep up the hunt Kathy!

Maryanne Ogrodowski, I am so glad we shop at some of the same places, because if Katie or I miss a great purchase, you don't! Thank you for the Christmas bag in 2002.

Janna Kuhns, Katie is just starting to break you in; look out! Janna, always remember to buy a purse big enough to hold your binoculars, so you can watch all the supposed hot spots — Pittsburgh, Key West, etc; orange you glad you can look into *Blairsville*?

Sarah Uncapher, I loved it when Katie told me that at Cardin's bridal shower vintage purses were used for the favors. I'll bet this was a great idea of your mom's that you and Katie Uncapher helped execute.

Kayla Kreuger, it will be fun for you and Katie to shop the market for both of your favorites when the two of you are in college – no matter how far apart you are.

And a special thanks to Whitey, my husband, for the high-quality pictures. Thank you for sacrificing your time to help me. It is deeply appreciated.

Introduction

The first purses were donned by the Crusaders and used between the eleventh and that thirteenth centuries to carry alms to be given to the poor. Some definitions of *purse* from *Webster's New World Dictionary* are "a small bag or container to hold small change, usually carried in a handbag or pocket; a woman's handbag; resources of money, funds or treasury or a sum of money; any baglike receptacle, such as an animals pouch, a seed capsule, or a covering for a gold club." Today, purses vary in sizes, shapes, materials, designs, and styles.

A purse is a private possession — personal, prized, a true portrait of a woman's personality. Some women use purses to achieve power, status, or style; others carry purses for special occasions and everyday use.

The allure of a purse is connected to this daunting question: what is hiding inside? Sometimes common items such as makeup bags, keys, calculators, wallets, cell phones, brushes, hankies, glasses, pills, and more are put in purses; other times people use purses to tote around some of life's little items whose meanings may be a bit more ambiguous. Sometimes, I think what is inside can date the owner!

Remember the TV show *Let's Make A Deal*, which had Monty Hall as the host? My favorite part of the show was when he would request a woman in the audience to search for the wildest or wackiest item she carried in her purse. If she could retrieve the item, he had a prize for her.

As a little girl, I delighted in playing dress up, as so many of us did. I used to use my mother's and my grandmas' beloved bags. My grandmother Ault had a bag for the change of each season and a good purse for special occasions. That purse she kept wrapped in paper, and she stored it in a chest of drawers in her home, upstairs. To this day, I wonder what happened to it. It's a special 1940s beaded bag. I truly thought it was the most beautiful purse I had ever seen. The beads were so alive, so sparkly.

Purses are sometimes featured in *Vogue* magazine's last page, titled "Last Look." The "Last Look" I remember with purses featured was in the January 2003 issue that had Sandra Bullock on the cover. This is always a great page in the magazine, because it features either vintage or vogue purses, jewelry, and shoes, every woman's loves!

The joys of collecting are numerous. The ownership and the actual handling and visual enjoyments are sure to bring a smile to one's face. Whenever one is shopping for a new find, or perhaps carrying a vintage bag that one owns, purses can cause conversation to stir.

The places to shop for purses are flea markets, antique shows, vintage clothing stores, second-time-around shops or thrift shops, antiques shops, and the Internet. I still like personal shopping more than using the electronic technology.

Remember: try to buy bags in usable condition. Check the frame, design, wear and tear, handles, fringe, tassels, attachments, and manufacturers' trademarks. When making a purchase, document the following information: where you bought the bag, when, its condition, whether it is in the original box, whether all accessories are included, whether the original tags are with it, and who the previous owner was or where it came from, if possible. Always document as much information as possible.

Whether one is just beginning to collect or one is an advanced collector, I suggest one buys what matches one's *purse*onality! Buy what is liked and wanted. Enjoy each and every purchase.

Finally, a strange twist; my husband, my friend, always tells me to "leave the purse at home!" However, I never leave home without a purse. Maybe he is just a taste too conservative.

Tips for storing your purses:

Do not wrap your purses in plastic or paper. Use acid-free paper. This can be found at art supply stores.

Do not stack purses; stacking can loosen beads.

Do not let your purses get wet or damp. This is critical if a purse is made with steel; steel rusts.

If you have the original box or bag, date the container.

Fun Facts about Purses

The first zippered bag, the Boldie bag, was made in 1923 and was designed by Hermés.

A 1956 *Life Magazine* cover was graced by Grace Kelly, who used a Hermés bag to hide her pregnancy. In today's entertainment industry, if a pregnant actress must disguise her condition for a role, a well-placed bag is still a way to do it.

Leather shortages after WWII insprired Gucci to use cane handles on his bags.

In the 1940s and 1950s a new plastic, Lucite, was used to create bags with box shape and style.

Travelers who used stage coaches or trains often carried carpet bags.

Nancy Reagan, Barbara Bush, and Laura Bush each carried designer Judith Leiber's bags for their husbands' Inaugural Balls.

The first mesh bags were made by goldsmiths and silversmiths. In the 1820s, frames were sometimes done in precious stones.

The company Whiting and Davis took charge of the mesh market in the teens of the 1900s.

Screen printing on mesh was in vogue in the 1920s. Mesh was not used in WWII due to the lack of metals. Copper also was used then. In the 1950s, mesh came back into fashion with a new twist.

A comment from *Godey's Magazine* in July 1886 said that accessories were becoming more daring and that "gloves with tiny purses in the palm for containing car fare are not strikingly new."

The Mandalion and the Whiting and Davis bag companies were both located in Massachusetts. In 1929, Whiting and Davis took Mandalion into its firm and Mandalion bags were not produced again. This was a sad loss due to the economy.

Purse parts include the exterior, lining, frame, attachments (for example, the fringe, beads, rhinestones, and more), and handle.

Becoming Beads

Black clutch with a flap that zips. The black lining has an open side pocket. This bag is hand beaded, and it is signed "Made in Japan by Bonni Int'l." 7¾" x 6¼". 1930s –1940s. $25.00 – 55.00.

Bag from the 1930s or 1940s, 11½" x 6". Signed "Bags by Jose, Hand Beaded in Japan." $40.00 – 90.00.

This navy purse is rather heavy. It is all hand beaded and sewn; the silver zipper reads "Prentice." 1930s – 1940s. $25.00 – 55.00.

This purse is lined in cloth and has a pocket that zips. The tag is white and hand sewn. It reads "Made in Czechoslovakia." This bag is 6½" x 6". 1930s – 1940s. $25.00 – 55.00.

Wonderful wood-beaded bag that was usually sold through Sears mail order catalogs. 1937 original price tag reads "$1.88." $18.00 – 48.00.

A great folk art piece from the 1930s that measures 9¼" x 6". $15.00 – 30.00.

Pea green purse with a silver zipper. Signed "Made in Czechoslovakia" on the inside pocket. The bag is 8¼" x 4¾". 1930s. $25.00 – 45.00.

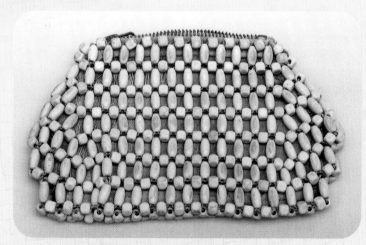

The cloth lining of this bag is worn. A tag, which reads "Made in Czechoslovakia," is hand sewn at the top of the lining. The purse is 3¾" x 6¾". 1930s. $15.00 – 30.00

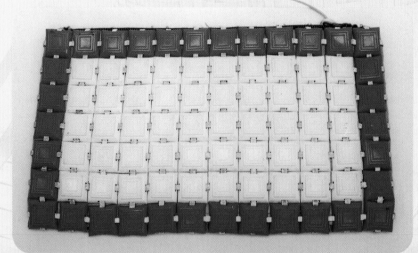

Plastic squares purse made under U.S. Patent No. 2,256,645, from the 1930s. Each square is ¾" and woven to the next with vinyl cording. This purse is 13¼" x 7½". $45.00 – 85.00.

Drawstring beaded bag
that is a 9" x 9" wonder
with a fun, fringed bottom.
1940s. $25.00 – 45.00.

This sort of reminds me of
traffic lights, or a raging, all-
night disco. The plastic beads
and the hanging fringe simply
swing from this large 9¼" x 11½"
purse. The handle alone is 16."
1940s. $15.00 – 25.00.

Absolutely artistic in
black, red, and white.
14½" x 12." 1940s.
$35.00 – 75.00.

A floral display for all to enjoy.
The bag measures 15¾" x 15¾",
and the handle is 6¾". The white
tag inside reads "Made in Hong
Kong." 1940s – early 1950s.
$18.00 – 38.00.

This 10¾" x 8¾" bag was "Made in the USA" in the 1950s. Very lovely. $70.00 – 110.00.

Purse signed By "Lumured Petite" that is 12¼" x 9". The single handle is 5¼". 1950s. $70.00 – 110.00.

Beaded bag with cream-colored ribbed satin lining. Signed "Corddi Bead" in gold; the rest of the writing is illegible. 1950s. $80.00 – 120.00.

Appealing 10" x 7" pansy purse from the 1950s. Signed something that looks like "Belgian Beads"; however, the signature is hard to read because it is fading. $80.00 – 120.00.

Charmingly quaint 1950s purse. The top of the purse has a matching gold-tone, white-enameled clasp. The bag is 9½" x 9" and is signed "Corddi Bead" in gold stamp; the rest of the name is illegible. $70.00 – 105.00.

Beaded bag on mesh nylon. There is a single beaded handle for this white wonder. The purse measures 9¾" x 9". It is signed "Cavias Beadette Lumared Made in USA." 1950s. $95.00 – 105.00.

A great purse for Easter. 9¼" x 9½". $45.00 – 90.00.

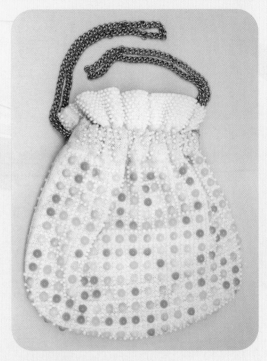

Lovely drawstring bag with lemon-colored beads. Made in Hong Kong. 1950s. 9¼" x 9½". $45.00 – 90.00.

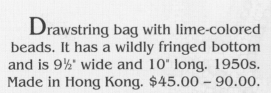

Drawstring bag with lime-colored beads. It has a wildly fringed bottom and is 9½" wide and 10" long. 1950s. Made in Hong Kong. $45.00 – 90.00.

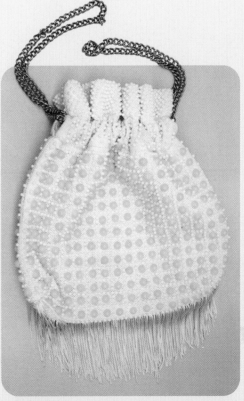

This 1950s charmer is 12⅛" wide, 8¼" tall, and has a 7¼" beaded strap with cloth lining. $50.00 – 95.00.

Small crystal and white bead diamond shapes on an off-white fabric. Signed "Lumored Cordel-Bead © Made in the USA Pat No 2,582,132," written in gold. I would fold over and use as a clutch. $50.00 – 95.00.

Beaded bag with single 6" handle finished with white beads and crystals. This purse is 9½" wide and 6½" tall. Signed "Cavair beads by Lumured Made in USA Pat No 2582332." 1950s. $48.00 – 88.00.

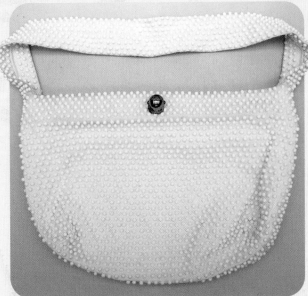

This is a beautifully beaded bag with a single 1½" wide handle. It is 10" wide and 7" high. 1940s. Unsigned. $40.00 – 70.00.

This great purse has white plastic double handles. Signed "Caviar Bead by Lumured Made in the USA Pat No 2582139," in a gold stamp. Measures 9¾" x 6¾". $40.00 – 70.00.

This 9⅛" x 7½" bag is signed "Cordel Bead By Lumored" in gold stamping. 1950s. $65.00 – 95.00.

Beaded bag in an every-other pattern. A flap is on each side, and a 12½" single handle finishes the purse. The bag is 7⅛" x 6½". A tag on the inside in red and blue reads "Designed by Mr. Jones. Made in Hong Kong." $55.00 – 85.00.

Pretty crafty clutch that is reversible. 10" x 8". 1940s. $45.00 – 75.00.

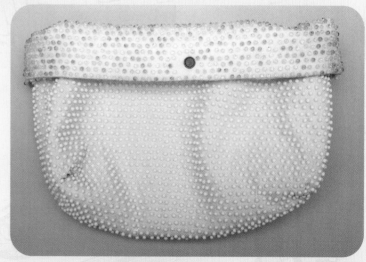

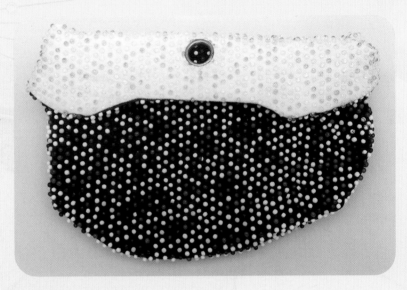

Reversible purse from the 1940s, 11" x 8". $45.00 – 75.00.

Reversible beaded clutch with one side in reds, yellows, blues, and green beads on a black fabric; the other side has white fabric with pastel beading. 10½" x 8½". 1940s. $45.00 – 75.00.

Cute beaded black purse, 1940s. $30.00 – 50.00.

The luck o' the Irish! This clutch is lined with an Irish green cloth. Very pretty, 1940s. Measures 8¾" x 5¾". $40.00 – 60.00.

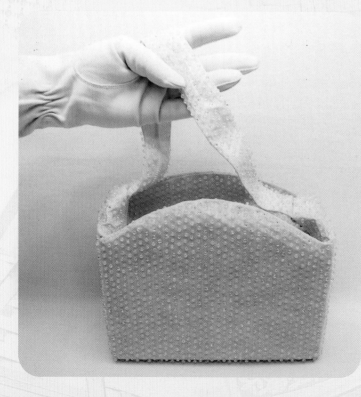

Elegant pink crystal beads are offset by a white fabric backing. This purse is stamped in gold tone on white lining, "Caviar Beadetts by Lumurus, Made in USA PAT No. 2," followed by letters that are illegible. This box-style bag measures 6½" x 8". The handle is 7½". Late 1940s. $45.00 – 95.00.

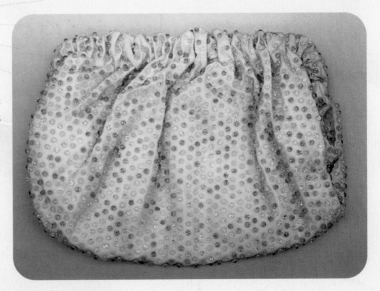

Very stiff to open and close clutch from the 1940s. Beads are in shades of lemon, mint, pastel blue, and pink. Measures 8¾" x 6". Unsigned. $35.00 – 65.00.

This delicate clutch has small crystal and white beads. The interior is also finished with the same design. The flap has a white zipper with a white plastic ring to close. The zipper reads "MURLEEN." The original plastic comb is still in the purse. 1940s; becoming worn. Gold stamped "Lumures MADE IN USA." $40.00 – 80.00.

Clutch gold stamped "Lumures MADE IN USA." 9" x 5¾". 1940s. $20.00 – 40.00.

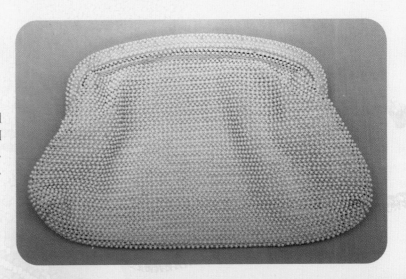

Beautiful brown beaded bag. Plastic on fabric. Measures 7¼" x 5½". 1940s. Note the double handle, and that the clasp is tie-like on the front. $35.00 – 65.00.

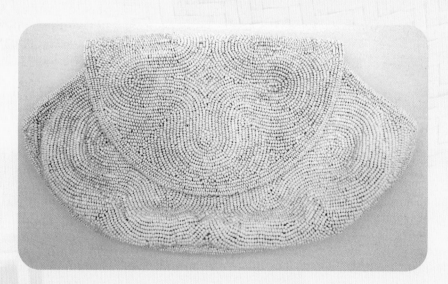

Inside label reads, in gold script, "Bags by Josef HAND BEADED IN FRANCE." The gold-tone satin lining is slightly discolored. The bag shows usage. The owner left a lace hanky in the bag. Brass clasp is signed "United." Weighted, measures 5" x 9¾". 1940s. $90.00 – 130.00.

Unmarked. Big, bold, and brazen colors are employed on this beaded bag with a Bakelite frame. Looks very Bohemian. Lined in a denim blue satin, worn. Appears to have had an inside pocket. Could use TLC. Measures 6¼" x 8¼". 1915 – 1920s. $375.00 – 475.00.

This beaded purse has a stunning needlepoint floral set on the front that is accented by ornate black beads. The purse has a black satin lining with a white satin tag that reads "Made in British Hong Kong." 10¼" x 7½". The handle is 5¼" and done in beads. $250.00 – 350.00.

This off-white clutch has a daring symmetrical geometric design. I don't know if it is signed inside or not, because I cannot open this bag! 1930s. 6" x 3¾". $70.00 – 105.00.

This purse is attached to a delicate chain. On the inside it has a nice, soft black lining and inner pocket. A silver-tone frame is used to finish both sides. 1930s – 1940s. 5½" x 4", with a 5⅛" handle. Unsigned, possibly made in Belgium. $45.00 – 75.00.

Clasp of mother-of-pearl in a gold-tone bezel set. Light gold satin lining with an open pocket. Gold-tone frame. The back has all off-white beads. The front has small white beads and a darker bead design around mother-of-pearl beads. Nine mother-of-pearl beads are missing. This bag measures 6" wide and 4½" high and has a 4¾" gold-tone chain-link handle. 1930s – 1940s; delicate. $70.00 – 130.00, as is.

A feisty flapper-style beaded bag. This is a real dance swinger with orange and black beads in a checkered pattern. A delicate drawstring rope is used as the handle. The lining is of matching orange silk. 6½" x 3¼". The fringe is ¾". Unsigned. 1920s. $130.00 – 180.00.

This flapper-style bag has shiny royal blue beads strung in a double loop. The lining is the same as the top of the bag. A drawstring rope is used for the handle. Measures 3½" wide and 8¾" long, and has 2¾" of beaded fringe tassel. 1920s. Unsigned. $155.00 – 205.00.

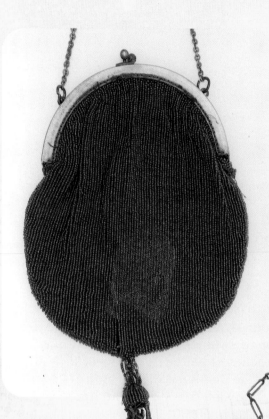

This beaded bag needs some TLC, because it shows wear and usage. The gold-tone frame resembles brass. The tassel measures 4½". The purse is 6¼" x 8", with a 3¾" chain handle. 1900s – 1920s. $155.00 – 205.00.

This beauty has a tapered, drape-like outline. A row of blue looped beads is hand attached to gold cloth. Frame is stamped on both sides; however, it is hard to read and says, "Made in Czechoslovakia." 1900s. $170.00 – 230.00.

This beaded bag has a missing frame, and there is a design on both the front and the back of the bag. The purple cloth lining has an open side pocket. 6½" x 6¾", with 1⅛" of fringe. 1900s. $145.00 – 195.00.

Hand-beaded bag with a drawstring to close. The drawstring goes through small brass hoops that are all hand sewn. Beads in black and silver. Flexible fringe at the top and bottom in double loops. Measures 9" long and 6¾" wide. Some fringe is missing. Purse is lined in black muslin. This bag was used. Unmarked, 1900s. $205.00 – 275.00.

Hand-beaded bag with black beads in double loops attached to the fabric. The gold-colored chain is in the double loops. Bag is lined in black cloth. Measures 7¾" high and 6¼" wide. Unmarked, 1900s. $205.00 – 275.00.

Coin bag or vanity compact. All hand beaded in cooper beads with flexible loops. The top is silver and very detailed. A chain is attached, with a loop for a finger or to attach to a belt. When opened, you can see yourself in the original, round mirror. Unmarked, 1900s. $145.00 – 165.00.

Weighted drawstring bag with missing drawstring. Hand crocheted, with cut steel beads applied. Measures 4¾" wide and 6½" high. Unmarked, 1900s. $135.00 – 165.00.

Cut steel beads are on this handmade bag. Bag is lined in peach cotton. Measures 5¾" wide and 5½" high. Unmarked, 1900s. $100.00 – 120.00.

Cut steel beads on the bag. Silver-tone frame with a 5¼" handle. Inside the bag, the lining is hand stitched; the pattern is a dainty black and white check pattern. Flexible fringed sides with the right side fringe missing. Bottom fringe is double looped. Unmarked, 1900s. $190.00 – 240.00.

This beaded beauty is 9¾" high and 7¼" wide, with a 5¼" double-loop chain. These cut steel beads are in a muted color floral design on the front and back. The bottom has single beaded fringe. Unmarked, 1900s. $950.00 – 1,350.00.

This three-tone plastic-beaded bag is from the 1960s. Measures 14" wide and 12" high. The front is tri-colored, but the back is done in all black beads. The handle is 14", and the bag is lined in black fabric. The silver zipper that is on the pocket is signed "UKK." The opposite side is open. The white satin tag reads "MADE IN HONG KONG" in red thread. $47.00 – 77.00.

Cut steel beads in a square form a design with T-shaped open spaces. 8½" x 5½". The chain is 9¾" long. Single loop fringe is attached to the flap. At the bottom is a beaded ball of cut steel beads. Hand crocheted. Unmarked, 1900s. $150.00 – 200.00.

Really red beaded bag from the 1950s. Unsigned. Measures 10¾" wide and 7¾" high. The double handles are 6½". The red satin lining is great. Katie carries this occasionally. $40.00 – 80.00.

Black beads of the early 1950s are shown off by the black Lucite frame backed with gold tone. The closure has a gold-tone snap. The single handle measures 6". Bag is lined in black fabric. One side pocket is zippered, with a white tag that reads "TARA ORIGINAL MADE IN HONG KONG." The other side has an open pocket. Quite heavy and large. Measures 14¾" wide and 9¼" high. Early 1950s. Katie uses this in the winter months. $50.00 – 90.00.

The white Lucite frame bordered in gold tone shows this eggshell beaded bag in high style! The lining is done in the same color as the purse. Bag is all hand stitched. Open inside pocket has a white tag with black stitching that reads "HAND MADE IN HONG KONG La Regal." $45.00 – 85.00.

The great single handle is 14¾". Seven sections of seven gold-tone links alternate with six sections of eight plastic beads to create a great shoulder length. Crocheted bottom and a completely crocheted back. Lined in vinyl with a small hand-sewn white tag with red stitching that reads "MADE IN JAPAN." The clasp is a gold-tone twist closure. The bag measures 8¼" wide and 7" high. 1940s – early 1950s. $25.00 – 45.00.

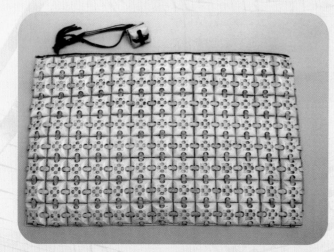

These 1" plastic squares are connected by leather. The 6" black leather zipper has a square attached as a zipper pull. The purse measures 13¾" wide and 8½" high. It is lined in black satin and has an open pocket on each side. A white tag with red print is attached to one pocket and reads "Plastic flex Trademark US PA 2256 645." 1940s – early 1950s. $35.00 – 55.00.

This petite beauty has a red Bakelite frame. The beads are colorful white, green, blue, and yellow. The red background is great for the beads. The purse is lined with red fabric. The open inside pocket is bordered with a gold-tone cord. A tag is sewn on the pocket. The bag is stamped, but the words are written with Asian characters. I can read the words "Poppy Bag." 1940s – early 1950s. The bag measures 7" wide and 6½" high. $35.00 – 75.00.

This beaded bag measures 9¾" wide and 7¼" high. The single, matching handle is 4½". The fabric lining is off-white. The pocket is open inside and stamped in gold; however, the writing is illegible. The crystal and aqua beads are accented with a gold-tone frame and twist closure. 1950s. $45.00 – 85.00.

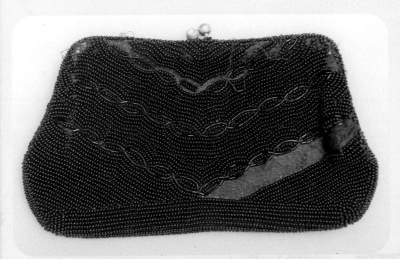

Small black beads and tube beads combine to create a figure eight design. A rhinestone is bezel set, and has baguettes on the twist closure. The bag is lined in black satin and has an open inside pocket. A white tag in gold lettering reads "MADE IN JAPAN." Purse measures 7½" wide and 4⅛" high. The bottom right side of the purse has beads missing. The back of the bag is without the design and just has small beads. 1930s – early 1940s. $28.00 – 48.00.

Flexible double loops are attached to the small beads on this bag. Lined in red satin, this early 1900s bag has a gold-tone chain with a wrist band. All handmade; measures 4½" wide and 5¼" high. $225.00 – 375.00.

Beauty is in the eye of the beholder, and I think this is beautiful. The silver-tone frame is unmarked. The lining is off-white satin and has an open side pocket. Attached by a white satin ribbon is a mirror backed in white satin. It has a white satin label that is sewn in gold thread and reads "Christiana." Measures 9" high and 6½" wide; the silver-tone link chain is 23¼". Late 1800s. $935.00 – 1,335.00.

Elegant Evening

This purse has gold flexible sequins, black fabric trim, and a satin cording double handle. The lining is done in a soft ivory and has an open side pocket. The bag is marked "DELILL MADE IN CHINA" and measures 8" wide and 7" high. 1970s. $25.00 – 65.00.

Black fabric clutch with a rhinestone bow in the center. An optional rope handle measures 18½" and is made from rayon cording. The bag is lined in black nylon and has a single side pocket. Marked "Created in China exclusively for Avon." 9¼" wide and 5½" high, 1970s. $35.00 – 65.00.

Goldilocks, what pizzazz! This is lined in dark beige satin and has a center pocket. The metal frame is gold tone and the bag has a crown clasp. The bag is signed "IBU" and is from the 1970s. Measures 8" wide and 4½" high. $35.00 – 65.00.

Burgundy suede handbag with a detailed decorative gold-tone frame. This purse measures 8¾" and 5½" wide and has a 14½" single chain handle. It is unsigned. Late 1960s – 1970s. Simply classic. $40.00 – 80.00.

Bag has a double gold-tone chain and a 2½" decorative gold-tone bar attached to the front. The frame is done in gold-tone, and the purse has a snap closure. Measures 7" wide and 7½" long. Mid-1960s – early 1970s. $35.00 – 65.00.

An elegant floral design graces this black satin beauty. The lining is gold satin with linen behind the satin, all hand sewn and knotted to the frame. Frame is ornate, with jade in a bezel setting. The top clasp set off of the frame's center is also done in gold tone with jade. This bag looks to be from France and measures 5½" wide and 5¾" long. Unmarked, late 1800s – 1910. $230.00 – 300.00.

This would cause envy at any Christmas party! "MM" signature in gold. Double inside pockets hold a comb and mirror in one, and a coin purse (attached by chain to the frame of the bag) in the other. The purse is lined in gold satin and has an emerald green satin outer. A gold-tone clasp to close. A bow is on the bottom of this purse. Measures 6" wide and 7¼" long. 1950s. $65.00 – 95.00.

Emerald green satin purse lined in a gold satin. A gold-tone leaf with small crystals and rhinestones makes up the clasp. Great for St. Patrick's Day! 1950s. Signature in gold, a lamp of radiating rays marked "After Five R." Made in USA. $55.00 – 85.00.

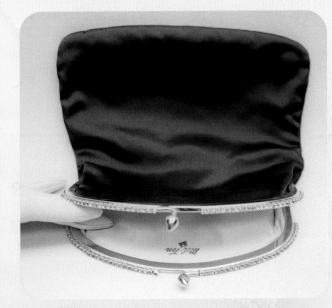

Signature in gold, "Mel-Ton" followed by a design of a purse dangling from the *l* in the *Mel*. This clutch is framed in gold tone with rhinestones. Lining is done with a light gold satin. The bag measures 8¼" wide and 9¼" long. A Taurus or a Gemini (like my mother) would look great carrying this in the month of May. 1950s. $65.00 – 95.00.

Gold-tone evening clutch bag with an aurora borealis clasp. It is lined in black satin. The gold-tone chain measures 4¾", and the purse is 8¼" wide and 4¼" high. Unmarked, 1960s. $35.00 – 50.00.

Metallic gold-tone bag with a gold-tone rope handle. The purse is lined in black satin with a gold-tone crown clasp. The handle is 5". The bag measures 9" wide and 4½" tall. Unmarked, 1960s. $35.00 – 50.00.

This gold-tone bag is lined in nude beige satin. The inside is divided and is stamped "HLUSA" in black. The metal frame is gold tone, and a gold clasp is inset with pavé rhinestones. 1960s. $20.00 – 40.00.

Clutch (above, top), 1960s. The lining is sand colored. There is an orange-bordered yellow sticker stamped "Andé." The bag is silver tone and has a gold-tone clasp on the front. The silver chain handle is 15". A 1½" chain has a ½" silver bar that connects to it. $25.00 – 45.00.

Metallic silver-tone 1960s clutch (above, bottom) measures 10½" wide and 4¾" high. The handle of cloth is 4¾". The bag is lined in black vinyl with a dotted design. A silver-tone flower with a large center rhinestone is used for the clasp. Unmarked. $25.00 – 45.00.

Evening clutch in silver tone and lined in black vinyl. This clutch measures 8" wide and 4¾" high. The silver link chain is 3¾". This is finished off with a silver-tone crown clasp. Unmarked, 1960s. $25.00 – 45.00.

Black satin purse from the 1960s. Tailored, this never goes out of style. Measures 10½" wide and 5¾" high. The handle is a 4½" gold-tone rope. The gold-tone frame borders the black satin. The black satin is gaped to the frame. Unsigned. $20.00 – 40.00.

Seeing double! Sequins in pink, white, blue, and black. Lined in black satin, the purses each have an inside pocket. The bags have silver-tone snap clasps. The single handles of black sequins are 3". Unsigned, 1950s. $35.00 – 65.00.

This is marked "Exclusively for LA REGALE HONG KONG LT HANDMADE" and was made in the 1940s or early 1950s. I love this clutch! It has colored rhinestones on a gold fabric, and a border of small gold-tone beads. The light gold satin lining has an open inside pocket. The back of the clutch is gold satin fabric that has a delicate floral design. The purse measures 9½" wide and 4¾" high. $75.00 – 115.00.

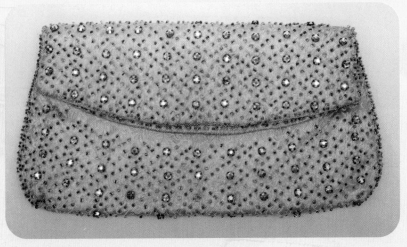

Black beaded evening bag. It has a finished beaded ball on a zipper to close. The purse is lined in black satin and has an open side pocket. Weighted. Purse is excellent quality! Measures 10⅛" wide and 7" high. Unsigned, 1940s. $135.00 – 175.00.

Inside of this superior black beaded box, you will find a full-sized mirror. The bag is lined in black satin and has an open side pocket. This has quality craftsmanship and is weighted. 1940s. It measures 8" wide and 4¾" high and has a handle 1⅛" wide. This bag is my mom's. $135.00 – 175.00.

This 1940s bag measures 7½" wide and 4½" high. It is unmarked. It has iridescent dark blue beads on dark blue velvet with a blue-purple satin lining and an open side pocket. The top is finished in gold roping. The snap reads "pull proof RAU F CO." The back side of the handle is lined to match the purse's interior. A dark blue satin coin purse lined in buttercup satin matches the purse. $135.00 – 175.00.

Black beaded clutch with a diamond pattern. 1950s to early 1960s. Measures 8¾" wide and 4¾" high. The inside is lined in black satin and has an open side pocket. The white tag reads "MADE IN HONG KONG" in gold thread. $45.00 – 65.00.

Hand-beaded clutch. The front flap has a floral swirl design and a border of three-bead groupings in a running series. The bottom of the clutch has a three-bead series that matches the back. The purse is lined in black satin and has an open side pocket. Unmarked, 1950s – early 1960s. A silver snap reads "PAT 201430-22 NEWEY." Bag measures 9½" wide and 5¼" high. $45.00 – 65.00.

The 4½" single handle on this bag is so fitting! This purse is finished on the top with beads, and the back of it is lined in black satin. The flap design has beaded flowers in a diamond pattern. The bottom has beads raised off the fabric in a ribbon design. A silver snap reads "KANE — M-M." The white satin tag on the open inside pocket reads "MADE IN HONG KONG" in red thread. 1950s – early 1960s. $45.00 – 65.00.

The roped handle on this bag measures 20¾" long. Black beads on the flap are bordered with raised beads. Two-bead groupings are hand threaded on the bottom and the back. The gold snap reads "BRAND T. K*K." The bag is lined in black rayon. The tag is hand sewn on the open pocket and reads "100% rayon MADE IN CHINA." 1960s – 1970s. Measures 8½" wide and 5¾" high. $30.00 – 40.00.

Hand-beaded purse with a raised grouping of black beads in a diamond pattern that has swirls set inside the diamonds. This purse is lined in black satin, with a white tag sewn on an open pocket. The tag reads "MADE IN HONG KONG." The bag measures 7¾" wide and 5½" high. Weighted. 1950s – early 1960s. $75.00 – 115.00.

Weighted beaded bag. Great detailing. The front and back have the same design of silvery white beads. The bag has a silver frame and silver chain. The chain is linked tubes and measures 6¼". The purse is lined in white satin and has an open inside pocket. White tag reads "hand beaded in Hong Kong WALBAE." The bag measures 7¼" wide and 4½" high. 1950s. $75.00 – 115.00.

Mellow yellow clutch with raised gold beads in palm trees. Groups of one and three beads are hand threaded in an alternating pattern. A flap on the clutch is bordered in three-bead groupings. A silver-tone snap reads "NEWEY PAT 201430-22." Inside flap is grapefruit-colored satin. One pocket is open and holds an original mirror. The other is zippered and has a hand-sewn tag that reads "MADE IN HONG KONG." The purse measures 8⅛" wide and 5" high. 1950s – 1960s. $75.00 – 115.00.

Clutch beaded in multiple teal colors and gold. The background is of green sequins. This bag is lined in emerald satin and has an open inside pocket. The silver-tone frame has a silver clasp inset with rhinestones. The purse measures 10¾" wide and 5" high. Unmarked. This great design is from the 1950s. $65.00 – 105.00.

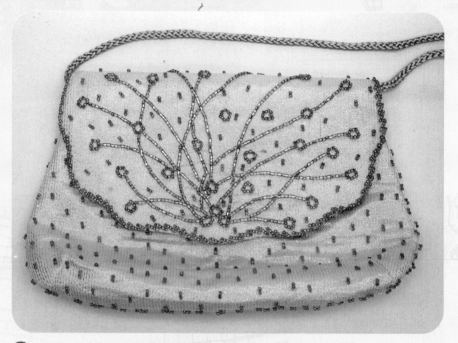

Small round and barrel-shaped beads are arranged in a spray design on the fabric of this bag. The flap is bordered with gold-tone bead clusters. The back design is made up of small gold two-bead clusters hand knotted to the fabric. The purse is lined in a light gold satin and has an open inside pocket. A white tag is sewn on to the pocket and reads "La Regale LTD. Handmade in China." This bag measures 9⅛" wide and 6¼" high. The gold rope handle is 22¾" long. 1970s. $30.00 – 50.00.

The fabric handle on this purse measures 8¼". On the flap of the bag, multicolored beaded flowers blend with an embroidered vine. The back of the purse is plain. Th lining is of the same material as the purse. Inside is a zippered pocket. A silver-tone snap closes the bag. This purse measures 10¼" wide and 6⅛" high. 1940s – 1950s. $40.00 – 70.00.

Silver sequined clutch, all handmade. Sequins are bordered by small silver beads. Bag is lined in off-white fabric and measures 8" wide and 4½" high. The tag sewn on the inside pocket reads "MADE IN CZECHOSLOVAKIA." Late 1930s – mid-1940s. $30.00 – 50.00.

Drawstring bag in gold-tone sequins and beads. The trim is finished in beads, with the top being a single-strand border of beads. Handmade, done on a netted fabric backed with light gold satin. Drawstring measures 4¾". This bag measures 6¾" high and 5" wide. Unmarked, 1940s. $30.00 – 50.00.

Coin bag in purple satin. Lined in purple satin. Frame is gold-tone with black, gray, and yellow painted design. Measures 4½" wide and 3¼" high. Unmarked, 1940s – early 1950s. $15.00 – 20.00.

Black velvet clutch lined in black rayon. The tag sewn on the open inside pocket reads "Claire Made In China." The purse has a gold-tone frame and a 24¼" gold-tone staple chain. The chain is optional. The bag measures 5¾" high and 6" wide. 1980s. $18.00 – 28.00.

Black fabric purse with a black rhinestone clasp. The double handle is roped cloth. This purse is lined in black fabric and has an open side pocket. It measures 9" wide and 6¼" high. Unmarked, 1940s. $30.00 – 50.00.

A blue, blue clutch with a wonderful flap! The flap has white cabochons in figure eight designs. Small rhinestones are set between each pair of beads. The back of the clutch has a series of eighteen three-bead groupings of hand-threaded small white beads. The purse is lined in dark blue satin and has an open pocket. The bag measures 9¾" wide and 5½" high. 1940s. $48.00 – 78.00.

Weighted rhinestone clutch. This is such a great example of the dazzling 1950s. The bag has three compartments. One holds a mirror, original comb, and lipstick holder. This compartment opens into a cigarette compartment, which in turn opens into a compact compartment. Rhinestones on the outside of the purse are arranged in a shooting star design on gold-tone metal. This accenting is complimented by the black felt. The purse's design is finished in a border of gold roping. The gold mesh handle is 5½". This bag measures 5¼" wide and 3" high. Unmarked. $135.00 – 175.00.

Silver glitter, great for a New Year's Eve Party! A bezel-set rhinestone is set in the center closure of this purse. The silver tube chain is 5". The purse measures 9" wide and 4¾" high. 1960s. $45.00 – 75.00.

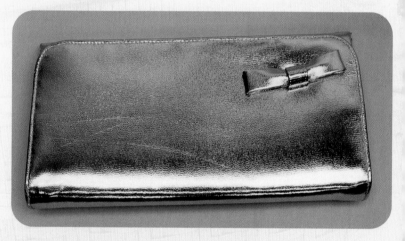

Silver-tone clutch from the 1970s, with a bow in the corner. This clutch is lined in off-white satin. It measures 9⅛" wide and 4¼" high. I wonder if Farrah carried this beauty? $25.00 – 45.00.

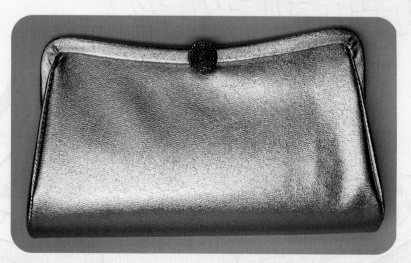

Good as gold! This clutch is a golden example of the 1970s. It measures 9½" wide and 4¾" high and has a gold-tone round clasp. $25.00 – 45.00.

This black patent leather clutch has a gold-tone twist clasp. Inside it has a place for a chain to be connected, so it can also be carried as a shoulder bag. The chain is missing. The lining has a interesting pattern of small squares in a red, white, and blue nautical design on an off-white fabric. Measures 12" wide and 5" high. 1960s. $35.00 – 65.00.

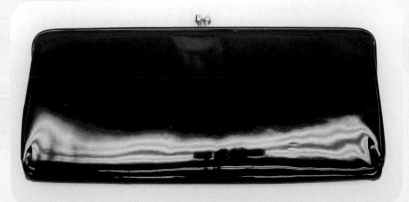

This glitter bag from the 1970s measures 8¾" wide and 4½" high. The silver-tone link chain is 5". The closure is a rose with a bezel-set rhinestone of medium size. There is circular silver glitter pattern on the purse fabric. It would be fun to use this bag during the holidays. The black satin lining is unmarked. $45.00 – 75.00.

Black velvet bag from the 1940s. Double handles measure 5"; the bag is 9" high and 7½" wide. The purse is lined in black satin and has an open pocket trimmed on top with gold rope. The closure is raised and has a gold-tone swirl design that holds a small rhinestone in a bezel setting. Unmarked. $35.00 – 65.00.

German Silver & Silver

This purse is signed "GERMAN SILVER" on the inside frame. Large flowers are engraved on the frame. The bag measures 5½" wide and 4¾" long; the chain is 7¾". 1900 – 1910. $125.00 – 175.00.

This bag is signed "G. SILVER" on the inside frame. Flowers are on the inside and the center of the frame. The purse measures 3½" wide and 4" long., the chain is 12" long. 1900 – 1910. $95.00 – 125.00.

Unsigned bag, 1900 – 1910.
The frame has a floral
decoration. $75.00 – 115.00.

Cosmetic bag or coin bag
with a 3" handle. The top is
expandable to 2". The purse
is 3¾". An engraved design
on the top is a feather with a
floral center. Unmarked.
$145.00 – 185.00.

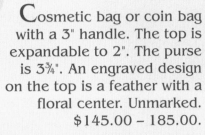

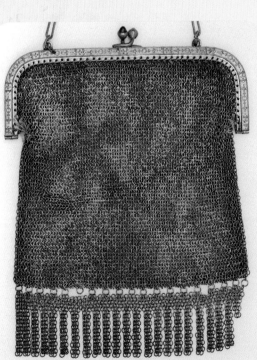

This is signed "GERMANY" on the
frame. This metal mesh bag
measures 4½" wide and 5¼" long and
has a 5½" chain. The tips of the clasp
have blue glass in them. The bag is
fully lined in a beige cloth. 1900 –
1915. $110.00 – 160.00.

Made from the early 1900s, this leather-lined bag measures 5¾" by 4¾" and has a 3" chain handle. The ornate frame is signed "GERMAN SILVER" on one side and signed "PAT MAY 7 1901" on the other. The bag is made of cut steel. Five steel balls that dangle from the bottom center are missing. The front of the purse is engraved "MEH." The back is the same as the front, but without the initials. This bag was my mother's grandmother's, is now mine, and one day will be Katie's. $160.00 – 220.00.

This is signed "German Silver" on both sides of the frame. The purse is made from steel, designed in loops. Five balls dangle from the bottom. The purse is 6⅛" wide and 4½" high. 1900 – 1910. $125.00 – 175.00.

Lovely Lucite

Unmarked late 1940s Lucite handbag looks like it could be by Llewellyn. The quality of the rhinestones glued to the frame is excellent. This bag most likely came with a feminine print, such as a picture of kittens, that was meant to be placed inside to be seen. $125.00 – 195.00.

The tag is marked "Original by Midas of Miami Handi-crafts Inc. Miami 47, FLORIDA." This 1950s beauty is made of Lucite and has white seed beads applied to it. There is a graceful needlepoint rose on the top and on the front. The bag has a quilted lining and measures 8" wide and 4¼" deep. $135.00 – 175.00.

The tag for this purse was glued in and is now missing. A wonderful example from the 1940s, this brown Lucite purse has a crystal clear rigid top. It measures 8½" wide and 4" deep and has 7" double handles. $125.00 – 175.00.

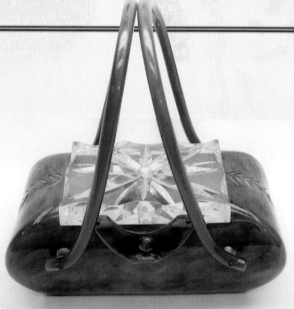

Signed "WILARDY US PATENTED." On the bottom inside of the purse, it is engraved "WILARDY." Tortoiseshell Lucite with brass is applied to the handles and the closure. When you open the purse, you can admire yourself in the full mirror inset in the inside lid. Exquisite! Measures 11" wide and 4" deep. 1950s. $200.00 – 300.00.

This is signed "Florida Handbags made in Miami" on a cloth tag. It measures 8½" wide and 3½" tall and is made of Lucite in a gold-brown color, with a clear top and matching clear handle. The top and handle have a design of a wildflower with leaves. 1950s. Unique shape. $125.00 – 165.00.

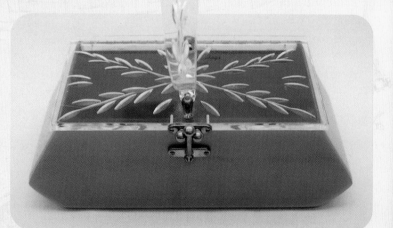

Signed "ORIGINAL RIALT of NY" on the brass hinge. This Lucite purse is silver gray and has matching handles and a crystal-clear top. The top has two large flowers on the sides of it, with a spray of leaves shooting across it. Four feet are made of clear Lucite balls. The bag looks to have been used heavily, and shows little signs of care. 1950s. $100.00 – 130.00.

It is hard to imagine that this is not signed. What a great woven metal bag! The gold and silver tones are set off with a tortoiseshell Lucite top with a clear handle. Katie carries this while shopping for vintage jewelry. $115.00 – 145.00.

Engraved "Majestic" on the gold satin lining of the inside lid. Silver- and gold-tone metals are in a woven design. The top matches the sides of the bag. Double gold-tone handles measure 3½". The bottom of the purse is gold-tone, and the bag measures 8¼" wide and 3¾" tall. It looks worn; little care was given to the purse. 1950s – early 1960s. $100.00 – 130.00.

Material Girls

There is an open pocket in each side of this clutch from the late 1960s. The outside of the purse is done in black velvet and has a vivid floral spray design made of gold beads and thread. The purse has black satin lining that has a white tag signed "Made in India" in black thread. The purse measures 7¾" wide and 4¾" high, and has a snap closure. $45.00 – 85.00.

On this evening shoulder clutch, gold threads, beads, and cabochons adorn black velvet. The bag is lined in black satin, and there is an open side pocket on the back interior of the clutch. The purse looks like it was made in India; however, it does not have a tag or signature. 3½" high and 4¾" wide. The snap closure is signed "KANE M." 1960s – early 1970s. $40.00 – 80.00.

This hand clutch opens to a great sand-colored lining. A coin purse holds a 1¾" x 2¾" coin bag inside, and a mirror and open inside pocket are found in this bag. The purse is embossed with gold threads, and has hints of deep red, butterscotch, and white against the purple-blue base. It measures 5¼" high and 4¾" wide, and the handle is 6½". The inside of the handle is finished in a sand-colored fabric. 1960s – early 1970s. $95.00 – 145.00.

There is a great detailed fabric used for this clutch, which has a celluloid elephant over the snap. A finger or hand grip is on the back. There is a black leather border around the flap. The lining is off-white fabric. A zippered center section has an open pocket with an original mirror in it. The mirror is covered on one side with fabric that matches the clutch. The mirror measures 2¼" high and 2¾" wide. The other side is possibly meant to hold jewelry. The purse is stamped "MADE IN JAPAN" in deep blue. 1960s. $85.00 – 105.00.

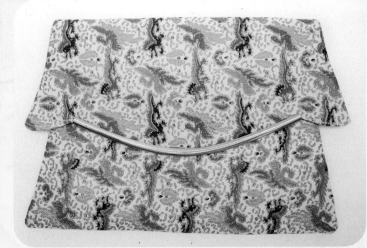

The signature in gold tone on the lining of this bag reads "Brite Mode." The purse has a light beige satin lining and an inside zipper signed "IDEAL" that falls under the top of the clutch. Bordering the fabric is a great gold-tone frame. The purse looks Oriental. Opened, the clutch measures 10". Closed, it is 6" long and 8¾" wide. Early 1940s. $45.00 – 95.00.

Pink metallic threads create the outline of the floral design on this 1950s clutch. The sides of the purse are hinged to open, and the bag is lined in off-white vinyl. A gold rope chain of 12" can be used or placed in the bag, which measures 10¼" wide and 6¾" tall. Unmarked. $35.00 – 55.00.

This is crocheted in gold and silver metallic thread, against a linen backing. The lining is off-white. The bag has a crocheted ring closure and measures 8½" wide and 6" tall. Unmarked, 1960s. $40.00 – 70.00.

Signed "MAJESTIC" in gold, this bag *is* majestic! It is 8½" wide and 5" high, and from the early 1970s. The flap opens to reveal a clutch. The flap and clutch are lined in black fabric. Inside, you will find an open pocket on each side. $25.00 – 50.00.

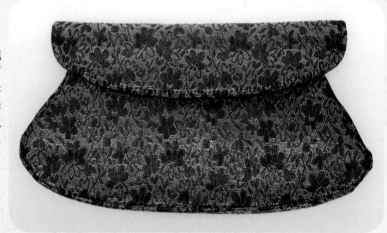

This is stamped "Britmode" in gold. From the early 1970s, it measures 8" wide and 4" high. Gold metallic thread on cream is offset with the metal gold-tone frame. The lining is gold-dotted satin and has a zippered pocket in the center. A pocket to hold a mirror is on the front of the bag. $25.00 – 45.00.

The floral fabric of this handbag is the same on its front and back. The double handle measures 4"; the purse is 13" wide and 10" high. Great for any summer garden party! The tag is signed "Margaret Smith Gardiner, Maine." This is my mom's purse. $60.00 – 100.00.

This green crocheted purse is attached to a silver-tone hinged frame and is lined in a light pea green fabric. It measures 9¾" wide and 7⅛" high, and the silver-tone link chain measures 6½". In this purse, I found a note on yellow paper that reads, "My mother, Helen Reed Wendell, crocheted this pocketbook in the 30s or 40s. I remember her making it." The note is signed "Phyliss Wendell Erickson." I left the note in the bag. $50.00 – 90.00.

The black fabric of this purse has black cut-steel beads in a heavy scroll design that reads "MOM." The fabric is attached by hand to the silver frame. I am surprised that the frame is unsigned. The satin lining is off-white with blue, red, yellow, and green stripes, and is wearing through to the gray fabric it is hand sewn to. This bag measures 5½" wide and 7½" high. 1900 – 1915. $130.00 – 180.00.

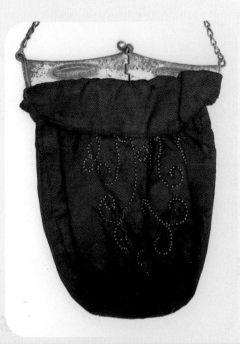

This is a box-type clutch from the 1950s measures 7¼" wide and 4" high. The double fabric handle is 3½". This purse is lined in peach satin and has an open side pocket bordered in gold cord. The original coin purse and mirror were found inside and and are now shown in this picture. The frame of the bag is done in gold tone, and the purse has a gold-tone clasp. Unsigned. $55.00 – 85.00.

This is a crocheted bag offered by catalogs in the early 1930s. The cut-out frame is off-white plastic, and has a chain of 3". The purse is 8¾" wide and 7¾" high. Unmarked. $45.00 – 75.00.

Marvelous Mesh

Silver mesh bag from the 1970s. A silver cloth lining has an open inside pocket. A white tag reads "MADE IN CHINA." The silver tag on the chain is signed "AE" on each side. A rope chain is 19", and the bag measures 8½" wide and 5" high. $40.00 – 80.00.

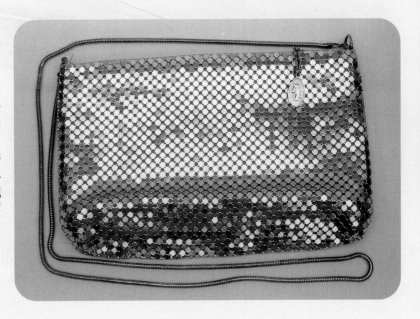

Off-white metal mesh purse with a metal frame trimmed in gold tone. The inside has a zippered pocket that has an open pocket in the lining inside it. A white tag reads "MADE IN CHINA." The 20½" rope chain matches the bag. The purse is 10¼" wide and 6" high. 1970s. $45.00 – 95.00.

Black mesh pocketbook from the 1970s has a nice gold-tone trim bordering the metal frame. The handle of black vinyl measures 19". The bag measures 10" wide and 6" high and has a zippered pocket inside. The inside is signed "Exclusive for Bueno. MADE IN CHINA." $40.00 – 80.00.

This white mesh bag has an open inside pocket. A pocket is also in the center. The bag has a white metal frame trimmed in gold. The metal rope handle is 19", and the bag itself measures 8¾" x 6¼". 1970s. $40.00 – 70.00.

Enameled metal mesh bag made sometime between the 1900s and the 1920s. A unique design of five metals in red makes a diamond pattern. The purse has an unsigned silver-tone metal frame. This purse measures 3½" wide and 5¾" long and has a chain of 6". A flapper-style hem finishes the purse. $95.00 – 135.00.

This enameled metal mesh bag was made sometime between the 1900s and the 1920s. This purse has an unsigned silver-tone metal frame and is brilliantly colored with blues and creams. It measures 3½" wide and 5¾" long and has a 6" chain. A flapper-style hem finishes the bag. $95.00 – 135.00.

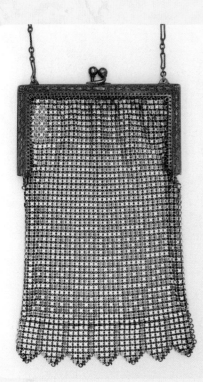

This is signed "MADALIAN MFG. CO. U.S.A." on the heavy ornate brass frame. Blues, browns, and off-whites make this enameled metal mesh a beauty. The dark pink lining is hand sewn. This bag measures 4¼" wide and 6¾" long. 1900s – 1920s. $200.00 – 300.00.

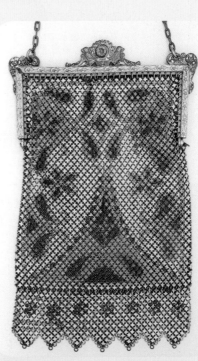

This bag is signed "Whiting & Davis Co." on both sides of the red enamel frame. A colorful bobcat design on this mesh bag is attention getting! The bag measures 5" wide and 6¾" long. 1900s – 1920s. $135.00 – 185.00.

Unsigned beaded bag with a cloth lining, finished in beading and attached to the frame with braided thread. A tie drop closure that hangs from the silver-tone frame measures 1". The heavily fringed bottom makes this a heavy bag. The purse measures 4¾" wide and 9" long and has a 6½" chain. 1915 – 1920s. $200.00 – 300.00.

The silver frame of this 1940s silver mesh purse is signed "WHITING & DAVIS CO. MESH BAGS MADE IN U.S.A." on both sides. The bag lined in white satin. The inside pocket includes the original mirror. The purse measures 4¾" wide and 5½" long and has a 5" chain. $75.00 – 115.00.

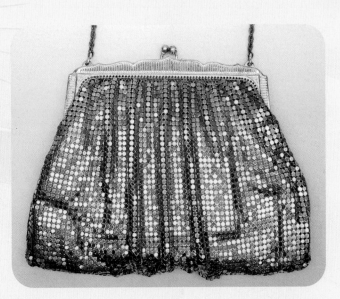

The frame of this gold mesh purse is signed "WHITING & DAVIS CO. MADE IN U.S.A." on both sides. The lining of the bag is gold satin. The inside pocket has the original mirror. The bag measures 4¾" wide and 6¾" long and has a 4" chain. 1940s. $90.00 – 130.00.

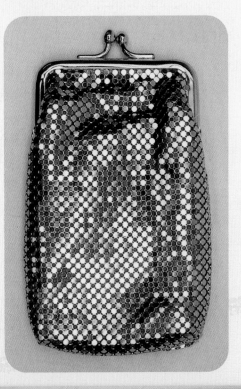

This cigarette case is stamped "Whiting and Davis INTERNATIONAL TM" on a gold-tone plate. There is also a white satin label that reads "Whiting and Davis INTERNATIONAL TM Made in China." What fun this case is to use today! It measures 5" long and 3½" wide. Late 1940s – 1950s. $35.00 – 55.00.

Wallet (left) with white satin label sewn inside that reads "MESH WHITING & DAVIS BAGS TRADEMARK MADE IN USA MFG." It is lined in black satin and measures 3" wide and 4" long. Late 1940s – 1950s. $25.00 – 45.00.

Compact (center), gold-tone mesh on one side and off-white enamel on the other. 1940s – 1950s. $20.00 – 40.00.

Cigarette case (right) stamped "Whiting and Davis INTERNATIONAL TM" on a gold-tone plate. There is a white satin label that reads "Whiting and Davis INTERNATIONAL TM Made in China." This case measures 5" long and 3½" wide. Late 1940s – 1950s. $35.00 – 55.00.

Both sides of the frame are signed "WHITING & DAVIS CO MESH BAGS MADE IN THE USA." This bag's gold satin lining matches its gold-tone outside. The clasp is made of rhinestones. This purse measures 3¾" wide and 4¾" long and has a 4¼" chain. Late 1940s – 1950s. $80.00 – 110.00.

Both sides of this purse's frame are signed "WHITING & DAVIS CO MESH BAGS MADE IN USA." Gold satin lining. Measures 3¾" wide and 4½" long and has a 4" chain. 1950s. $65.00 – 95.00.

This 1940s purse is unmarked. The gold-tone mesh bag has an inside pocket and a zipper closure. This purse measures 3½" wide and 4" long and has a 3½" chain. $55.00 – 75.00.

This gold-tone mesh purse from the 1970s measures 9¼" wide and 6½" long and has a 19½" chain. Unsigned. The zipper is marked "BEE" and has a clip for a key chain. How *BEE*utiful and simply stunning! $65.00 – 85.00.

This unsigned gold-tone metal mesh bag has a gold satin lining and an inside pocket. It closes with a zipper and measures 6¾" wide and 6½" long. It has a 2¼" double handle. 1950s. $55.00 – 95.00.

What a great celluloid frame and 6" chain handle on this bag. This purse is cloth and made to resemble mesh. The lining is done in black satin with an inside pocket. The bag measures 7⅛" long and 12¾" wide. 1940s. $55.00 – 95.00.

Alumesh purse with a celluloid frame and a 6½" chain handle. This purse has Beadlite enamel and is lined in black fabric. It has an open inside pocket that holds the original mirror. The tag reads "Alumesh Whiting & Davis Co. Bags MADE IN USA — Pa 18124." The tag is white satin with blue stamping. 1930s. $55.00 – 105.00.

Alumesh flamingo pink purse! It has pink Beadlite enamel and is lined in pink satin. It has an open inside pocket. The frame is celluloid and has a 4½" chain. This bag measures 8" wide and 4¾" high. Unmarked, 1930s. $55.00 – 105.00.

Unsigned Alumesh eggshell purse lined in white nylon. It measures 10⅛" wide and 9½" high. The 6¾" celluloid handle with the matching frame is a great example of 1930s style. $65.00 – 115.00.

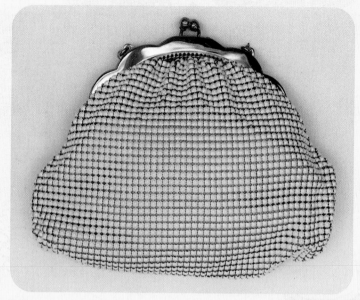

"Mesh Whiting & Davis Co. Trade mark manufactured MADE IN USA" is found in blue letering on a white satin tag inside this purse. The frame is stamped "Mesh Whiting & Davis Co. Bags 2908 Made In USA" on both sides. This mesh is done in eggshell and has a deep amethyst satin lining. The chain handle is missing from this purse. 1920s – 1930s. $85.00 – 125.00.

Silver-tone clutch with a cream-colored satin lining. The open side pocket has a tag in white satin with blue lettering. It reads "Mesh Whiting & Davis Co Bags Trademark REG MADE IN USA." The clasp is done in rhinestones. Weighted and of excellent quality, this bag measures 8" wide and 5" high. 1920s – 1930s. $70.00 – 120.00.

Cosmetic silver-tone mesh coin bag from the 1920s. The top opens and expands to form a pen-like structure around the mouth of the bag. The satin tag reads "Mesh Whiting & Davis Co. Bags Trade Mark MFG MADE IN USA." This bag measures 2¾" wide and 5" high and opens to 3¾"; it has a 4¾" silver chain-link handle. The top is etched. The lining is white satin. $95.00 – 145.00.

Gold-tone mesh three-piece set with the original ribbon and tag. Tag reads, "Another Y & S Original Style 598." The back of the tag also says, "Y & S Handbag Inc. NY, NY, NY Wholesale Handbag, Miami, FL." 1950s. $75.00 – 125.00 set.

One side of the frame of this silver-tone mesh purse is signed "Mesh Whiting Davis Co Bags." "MADE IN USA 9362" is found on each side. The silver-tone frame has a design of a crossed ribbon. A white satin tag is signed in the same manner as the frame. The inside has an open pocket. This bag measures 6" wide and 5" high, and the tube chain is 5¾". 1940s. This purse is my mom's. $85.00 – 145.00.

The white satin tag inside this reads "Whiting Davis Mesh Bag Co. Trademark Made In USA." This black mesh wallet is from the 1950s. It is lined in red satin and has an open-ended pocket and a snap coin pocket. $75.00 – 115.00.

This is either a child's gold mesh purse or a coin bag, made sometime in the 1920s or 1930s. Both sides of the inside frame are stamped "2962 MADE IN USA MESH WHITING DAVIS & CO. USA." The lining is done in a peach-colored satin and is hand sewn to the frame. The purse measures 3" wide and 2¾" high. $45.00 – 75.00.

This is a large gold mesh clutch from the 1970s. It measures 8⅛" wide and 4½" high. The frame has ⅛" of gold tone to border the flap. Inside, the snap is signed "US PAT 1519246." The white paper tag reads "MADE IN CHINA." $45.00 – 85.00.

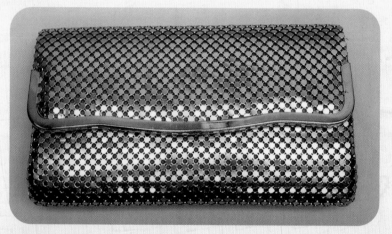

Eggshell mesh 1950s bag with a leather border and braided leather handles. This is a three-way bag. It has open pockets in each side of the bag. One side has a zippered pocket. The center of the bag closes with a gold-tone snap. The center is lined in white fabric, and the sides are lined in an off-white fabric. The handles measure 14", and the purse is 12" wide and 8¾" high. On the back of the purse is a side zipper the width of the bag. Because of its quality, it is surprising that this bag is unsigned. $65.00 – 105.00.

Precious Pearls

Cute, Canadian, and compact R. Gorwood seed pearl clutch from the 1940s or the early 1950s that measures 6¾" x 3¾". The zipper is signed "Nobiliay Hand Made." The interior has an off-white cotton lining; the anterior backing has a palm strap. Inset pearls complete the border. $15.00 – $35.00.

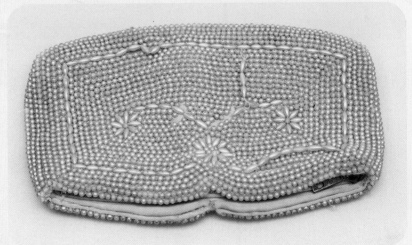

Heavy 1940s clutch with an off-white lining. Tag reads, "Made In Occupied Japan." 6½" x 4". $20.00 – 35.00.

Magnificently charming clutch with an excellent black diamondesque design on the outer front. 7⅛" by 3¾". 1940s – early 1950s. $20.00 – 40.00.

Elegant, rather feminine clutch. This dainty mid-1930s or 1940s charmer has a daring Deco design on the front. Five rhinestones help compose the angled bands on the purse's front. Unsigned. 7½" x 4". $25.00 – 45.00.

Try toting this clutch and you will feel like a star! Splendiferous starfish designs illuminate the front of the clutch. The exterior back portion is done in all white seed pearls in a swirly, ribbon-like design. 7⅛" x 5¼", 1940s. $25.00 – 45.00.

Flippant flowers abound on this flamboyant yet unostentatious seed pearl clutch. The original mirror remains intact inside the clutch. Pearls are sewn on to a nylon-type fabric. 6" x 4½", unsigned, 1930s – 1940s. $23.00 – 33.00.

Made in Japan masterpiece with an interior lining of cream-colored satin. The back is completed in solid pearls. This weighty purse is 7½" x 4¼". The silver-tone chain measures 5½". 1940s – early 1950s. $30.00 – 50.00.

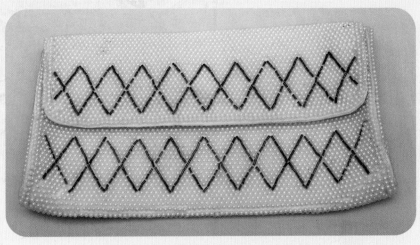

Grasping for the goods! This seed pearl purse can crisscross its way to one's heart on the double. *Double* as in the back matches the front! 7¼" x 5¾". 1930s. $30.00 – 60.00.

This stunning purse from the 1930s has a silver-tone snap and is lined in an off-white satin. It measures 7¼" x 5¾". Unsigned. $30.00 – 60.00.

An ocular feast, this purse from the 1930s is hand sewn. 5" wide and 4" tall. $35.00 – 65.00.

This plain Jane purse measures 5" wide and 4" tall. It is from the 1930s. $30.00 – 60.00.

Catchy clutch. Manufactured under the Ladies Handbag Code Authority 875055. It is signed "Hand sewn" and has the original mirror. Very heavy. The backing has a diamond design with swirls in the midsection. 5¾" wide and 3¼" high. $30.00 – 50.00.

This clutch has a unique symmetry of circles. It also has a golden ring so that it can be attached to a belt. 6" wide and 3¾" tall. $35.00 – 65.00.

The chain of this purse is MIA. White beads and off-white shading have been used to orchestrate an interesting, inset design. The front and back of the purse match. 4½" wide and 3¾" tall. Hand sewn. 1930s. $20.00 – 40.00.

This interesting clutch is hand sewn and has a fascinating zipper. The lining of the purse is brown. This bag is from the 1920s and has a palm grip. $25.00 – 55.00.

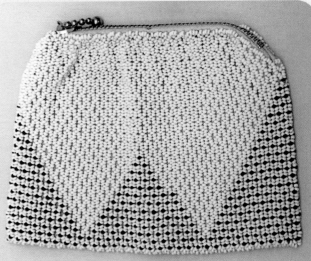

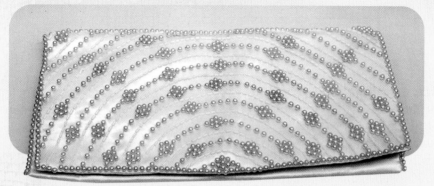

This clutch measures 9½" x 4½" and has a black satin lining. Signed "Exclusively made for La Regale Japan." $35.00 – 65.00.

The gold-tone frame of this purse has a snap closure. The purse measures 7¾" wide and 3¾" high and is hard sided and decorated with faux pearls. The inside has a zippered center pocket. Unsigned. 1950s. $25.00 – 45.00.

Faux pearl bag. Seven sets of five gold-tone beads in the same floral design adorn the front. The bag is lined in white satin and has an open center pocket. Gold-tone staple-like double chain measures 5¼". The purse measures 6" wide and 3½" high. Unmarked. 1940s. $35.00 – 65.00.

The purse has black beads on black fabric, and a black satin lining. The white tag reads "British made." The silver snap is stamped "MADE IN ENGLAND." This bag measures 7¼" wide and 4" high. 1920s – 1930s. On the back is a palm handle. The back design matches the one on the front. $50.00 – 80.00.

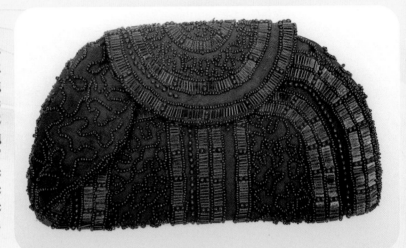

A small but mighty wonder, this seafoam green 1940s coin bag is signed "Delill, Handmade in Hong Kong." It measures 3¾" in diameter. $10.00 – 20.00.

Catchy clutch from the 1940s is dripping with pearls and is signed "Lane." 8⅛" wide and 5¼" tall. $18.00 – 38.00.

A seed pearl and sequin extravaganza! This evening clutch from the 1940s measures 5" x 9¾", and the silver snap is marked "Lane." $20.00 – 40.00.

"Handmade in Hong Kong" adorns the white tag in the left hand corner of the clutch's interior. Seed pearls and sequins are sewn on satin. 8¾" x 4¾". 1940s. $20.00 – 40.00.

Eye-stopping, petal-popping clutch of sequins and seed pearls in a floral design. Signed "I. A. Regale Product Made in Japan." 1940s. 8¼" x 4¾". $22.00 – 42.00.

This clutch has an 18" roped handle. The side pocket is open and has a black tag that reads "Daniele RN 64305." The black tag is accompanied by a white tag that reads "Hand Made in China." 8¾" x 4¾". $18.00 – 38.00.

Carolyne Barlon 1940s clutch. Made in China. 8¼" x 6". $25.00 – 40.00.

Simple yet elegant Sternmond Mann's of Canton, Ohio. Signed "Rechére by Walborg. Hand made in Japan." 1950s – early 1960s. 7¼" x 4¾". $20.00 – 58.00.

"K & G Charlet bag Made in Japan." Silver-tone clasp reads "H 33 H 333." A 9" x 5" delight. $21.00 – 41.00.

"Hand made in Hong Kong by La Regale Ltd." From the 1940s. This bag measures 6½" x 7". $22.00 – 42.00.

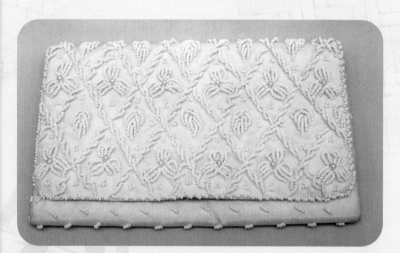

Made in Hong Kong flapped and beaded clutch. 8⅛" x 5". The silver-tone clasp reads "KANE MM." $18.00 – 28.00.

Splashy clutch of sequins and seed pearls. 6¾" x 7¼". Double satin handles are a posh feature of this 1940s work. $25.00 – 45.00.

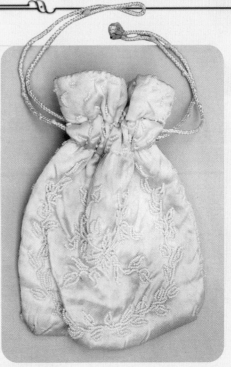

Delicate drawstring bag from the 1950s. A charming bag that would make a delightful wedding gift. 8⅛" x 5¾". $30.00 – 50.00.

Weighted 7" x 5" clutch from the 1940s or 1950s. The beads are applied to a muslin fabric. $35.00 – 75.00.

The tag is cut out of this purse from the 1940s or early 1950s. The original owner's hankie is still inside. Clutch measures 7½" x 4½". $40.00 – 75.00.

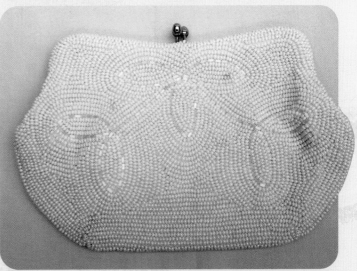

A lucky horseshoe pearl purse from the 1950s. 8½" x 4½". Unsigned. $35.00 – 75.00.

This Carlo Fellini bag was made in China. A 6" x 6" delight. The chain measures 23¼". 1970s. $30.00 – 50.00.

A beautiful box with a gold clasp closure. The interior white satin tag reads "Made in Japan exclusively for La Regale with Italian Beads." $70.00 – 120.00.

Rocking Reptile & Hand-tooled Leather

This leather clutch has whipstitched borders with the initials "E.G.M." stamped on the front in a scroll design. It opens to reveal bill holders on each side. One side has two open pockets, and the clutch has a sewn-in coin bag in the center. The coin bag has three snaps to close. The back of the clutch has a design of a large rose with five leaves and a small stem. This purse measures 7½" x 3¾". 1915 – 1930s. $105.00 – 135.00.

This is a very artsy-craftsy clutch made from leather, with a whipstitch border that has a very ornately detailed floral design. This design is repeated on each side. The purse opens via a zipper, and has a leather interior with two open pockets on one side. One pocket holds the original mirror. 7½" wide and 5½" tall. 1900s – 1920s. Unsigned. $105.00 - 135.00.

This purse has a whipstitched border and a leather interior. The purse is dsigned in an envelope style. One side is used for papers, and it opens to a pocket with two open, inside pockets. One pocket holds the original coin bag. The coin bag is 3⅛" x 2", and The purse is 8⅛" x 5". 1900s – 1920s. $120.00 – 160.00.

This quality handbag is rather heavy, and has an excellent detailed design. The purse is lined in leather and has a full open pocket on each side. There is a bag ID on the bottom left initialed "EDM." A silver barrel on a diamond frame is etched in a scroll design and twists to close the bag. 12" wide and 11½" tall. 1940s. Unsigned. $190.00 – 230.00.

This leather purse has a pocket with a whipstitched border. The front and back have the same design. A silver-tone circle with a 1¾" latch fastens the bag, and the purse has doubled leather handles. The leather of this bag is rather soft. Inside, the zippered pocket on one side opens to the other. This bag is rather detailed. 13" x 11". 1940s. $150.00 – 200.00.

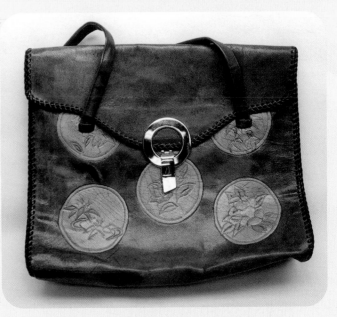

This hand-tooled leather bag is initialed "D.A.A." in the center. This was my grandmother's, Dorothy Allison-Ault. Grandmother Ault had exquisite taste. The double leather handles of this purse measure 17". A whipstitch border is employed on this purse, which has a zippered center. Inside there is a pocket on the side and three accordion-style folds. 1940s. Included in this set is a matching wallet, also initialed. Priceless.

Beautiful blonde purse made of hand-tooled leather. The bag has open pockets outside, one on each side. The inset center zipper opens to each side of the inside. A great floral print is used on this purse! 11" wide and 8½" tall, it has 9½" double handles. Unsigned. 1950s. $160.00 – 240.00.

This hand-tooled leather bag has a design on the front that matches the design on the back. The purse has a gold-tone twist snap closure. Blonde whipstitching is used for the purse's border. Inside, a zippered pocket is on one side, and an open pocket is on the other. 11" x 9", this bag has an 18" single handle. 1940s – 1950s. $130.00 – 160.00.

This unique single-handled leather bag uses brown whipstitching for borders and on the purse's strap. In the center, there is a hand-beaded large flower. Qué southwestern! 11¾" x 8½", this has a 14" single strap that is 1¼" wide. Unsigned. 1950s. $160.00 – 200.00.

Handbag with a gold-tone twist clasp that matches gold-tone framing. This bag is signed "Genuine Steer hide," and there is an open inside pocket that reads "Nylon Lined Nylon Stitched Mecker Joplin, Mo." This is in very nice shape. 11" x 5¾". 1940s – 1950s. $165.00 – 195.00.

This basket-shaped bag is of hand-tooled leather and is initialed "MJ." It is very nicely shaped. The top has brown whip-stitching and an inset zipper. The leather is rather stiff. This purse has a single, 3¾" leather handle and is decorated with imprints of flowers and leaves. 8⅛" x 9" tall. 1940s – 1950s. $155.00 – 185.00.

This handbag has a gold-tone frame and a snap on top. It is lined in beige and has an open side pocket. There are most likely matching shoes floating around out there, because the tag reads "Town and Country Shoes, TM REG." 8¾" x 8½". 1950s. $45.00 – 75.00.

This envelope-style handbag has a gold-tone twist closure. The purse is lined in purple ribbed satin. The bag has a center zipper and a 4½" double handle. It is 10" wide and 5½" tall. Mid-1950s – 1960s. Unsigned. $40.00 – 70.00.

This alligator bag has a whipstitch border and flaps that graduate in size. All flaps have a whipstitch border. Nice craftsmanship. Mid-1950s – early 1960s. 11" x 8¼". Unsigned. $95.00 – 145.00.

This alligator bag is lined in suede that matches an open inside pocket. This inside pocket is attached to a zipper pocket. A whipstitch border was used for the purse and the two flaps. The base has a twist closure. The flaps graduate in size. The bag is 9¼" x 6¾" and has a 13" single strap. Mid-1950s – early 1960s. $100.00 – 150.00.

An excellent-size purse from which to conduct business. This handbag is alligator and is rather stiff. The whipstitch border has a gold-tone base with a red twist-and-snap. The leather lining is neutral colored and has a zippered, inner pocket. The purse has a 15½" single handle and is 8⅛" x 6¾". It is signed "CLCO Genuine Alligator Made in Florida, U.S.A." $100.00 – 150.00.

"Genuine Alligator Florida Fashion MADE IN CUBA" is stamped on the suede lining of this bag. Strap is 10½", bag is 8½" x 5½". $120.00 – 170.00

This alligator handbag is lined in leather, and shows a head on the front and legs on the back. There is a whipstitch border on the purse flap. This purse has an adjustable 15" shoulder strap and measures 10" x 7¼". 1940s. Unsigned. $135.00 – 175.00.

This alligator handbag has a head and legs on the right front of the flap. It is very stiff on the top. The first flap opens to an open compartment, the second opens to another open compartment. White thread is used for the stitching. The purse has an 18" single strap and is 9¾" x 9½". Unmarked. 1940s. $175.00 – 205.00.

This alligator clutch is lined in leather and has whip-stitching around the flap and the base. It is 7¼" wide and 3¾" high. 1940s – early 1950s. It is signed "Genuine Alligator by HAL MADE IN CUBA" inside the flap. $75.00 – 95.00.

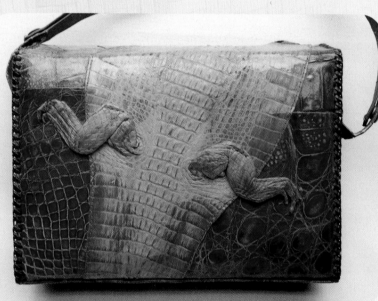

Rocking reptile from the 1940s. Tri-fold purse. $200.00 – 300.00.

Unmarked purse of faux snakeskin. This clutch is lined with a black cloth. Clasps are inside, which indicates that there once was a chain and this purse could also be worn as a shoulder bag. Matching gloves are darling. Early 1960s. $45.00 – 85.00.

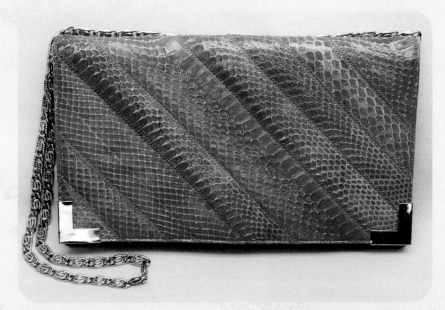

This envelope clutch opens to a copper-colored tri-fold leather lining. The exterior of this purse is copper-colored snakeskin. This clutch has a 14¾" gold chain and is 10⅛" x 5¾". "Bags are by VARON" in gold stamping. 1970s. $110.00 – 150.00.

This vinyl purse is meant to look like it is of red, black, green, and gray snakeskin. It is lined in bright red plastic and has an inside zipper pocket. The zipper pocket is lined in mustard yellow. The purse has a gold-tone frame topped by a gray bar. The bag measures 9⅛" x 9¾" and has a 4¾" handle. 1950s. $30.00 – 60.00.

This 11" x 8" purse has a 3" single strap. Imitation reptile is black and three shades of brown. A gold-tone frame is topped by a clasp and brown bar. This bag has a ribbed brown cloth lining and a zippered pocket that has an off-white tag. This is a Naturalizer handbag. The bottom is stamped "simulated leather 60092 733272." 1950s. $35.00 – 65.00.

This purse has two colored snakeskins that are great! I love this purse, with its 6⅛" handle. The purse measures 10⅛" x 7½". This is lined in off-white vinyl and has a zippered pocket. The black tag says "Brett's Feminine Fashion Johnstown, Pa." The opposite side has an open pocket with an original mirror in a white paper bag. Inside the purse, I found a grocery list and a car claim ticket from Smitty's Capital Parking, Main and Walnut Street, Johnstown, Pa. 1950s. $55.00 – 95.00.

Summertime Straw

Bahama blue round bag adorned with ocean blue and sea green flowers. Lining is ocean blue cloth. A silver, zippered pocket hides away the sun block. The double handles are braided straw. Mid-1940s – early 1950s. $45.00 – 95.00.

The original tag that hugs this Whidby bag reads "Whidby for Waikiki." This purse has straw lining. An original silk tag reads "handcrafted exclusively in the Philippines for Bags by Whidby, Inc. ADEL. GH." The price was left blank. This bag measures 9" wide and 5½" tall. It has double brown vinyl handles. Early 1950s. $60.00 – 110.00.

There is a bamboo handle for this straw purse that has a bone cloth lining. The bag measures 12½" wide and 5½" deep. A cloth tag reads "MADE IN JAPAN." Mid-1950s – early 1960s. $30.00 – 50.00.

Wicker wonder, with silk flowers to accent the top. This purse has double handles and measures 6½" wide and 3½" deep. Unmarked, early 1950s. $40.00 – 80.00.

This cutie could also be used as a sewing bag. There is paisley fabric on both sides of the purse, which measures 12" high and 10" wide. Unmarked, 1940s. $35.00 – 75.00.

This is signed "Fashion Imports MADE IN HONG KONG." The gold-tone double handles accent the shape of the bag. The clasp is belt buckle style and done in gold-tone to match the handles. The bag is lined in a cream-colored vinyl and has a gold, open side pocket sewn in. This purse measures 7" high and 8½" wide. $80.00 – 120.00.

This is a Jolles Original bag from the 1950s. The wood is woven. The top is decorated with small silk flowers and mesh. When the purse is opened, the lime green felt lining gets your attention. This purse measures 9¾" long and 4" deep and has a 5¾" handle. The handle is topped with a citrus-colored velvet ribbon and bow. Tropical! $95.00 – 150.00.

Mid-1940 – early 1950s. The square shape is stately. Double handles are gold encased. They measure 5¼". There is tapestry on each side of this handbag. The vinyl lining in a soft salmon color and has a long pocket on one side and a change pocket on the other. A tag on the long pocket reads "MADE IN HONG KONG." $60.00 – 90.00.

Woven straw bag, 1950s, "MANTESSA HANDMADE IN HONG KONG." Double straps are brown leather with matching snaps. This bag has a gray vinyl lining and a side pocket that is the width of the purse. The purse itself measures 11½" wide and 8" deep. $55.00 – 85.00.

The ivory-colored Lucite front of this purse measures 5½" wide and 2½" high. The 5" wide, 3½" high handle and the top of the bag are finished in Lucite. The lining is white cloth that has a pattern of ovals in earthy tones. The purse also has silver zippered pocket that has a slightly stained vinyl lining. The purse is signed "Handmade in Hong Kong Exclusive Design By Stylecraft Miami." 1940s – early 1950s. This bag measures 10" wide and 9" high. $75.00 – 115.00.

Tortoiseshell Lucite double handles top this 1950s purse that has a woven straw design. The handles measure 5" wide and 3½" high. This bag has a cream-colored vinyl lining and a side pocket with a gold-tone zipper. It is signed "Hand Made British Hong Kong" and measures 12½" wide and 9½" high. $75.00 – 115.00.

Down by the seashore! I love this purse. Signed "Princess Charming by Atlas Hollywood Fla MADE IN HONG KONG" on the side pocket of the purse. Double tortoiseshell Lucite handles are attached with gold-tone hinges. This bag has a gold-tone matching closure. Seashells are enclosed in plastic, and the display is bordered with gold-tone rickrack. Lined in a light coral vinyl, this straw purse has a middle section and a zipper.
1950s. $85.00 – 135.00.

"MADE IN SPAIN" is stamped on the wooden interior. This is a late 1940s bag measuring 12" high and 11½" wide. The single handle is 3½" high and 5½" wide. On the front is a 9" lone silk flower with two small flowers on each side. This is made of heavy woven straw. $70.00 – 110.00.

This bag would look great carried by a woman wearing a large floppy sun hat and great sunglasses. From the 1950s or early 1960s, this bag measures 10¾" high and has a fan shape. Double handles. Vinyl lemon-colored lining gets you in the ocean sands mood. $60.00 – 100.00.

Outstanding bag! Signature on tag says "AN ORIGINAL CREATION by Midas of Miami Handcrafted Inc. 47 fla." The purse is 12¼" wide and 9½" high. The gold-tone handle is 8⅛". The lining is gold tone, and the bag has an inside zipper pocket. This speaks for itself! $120.00 – 140.00.

Bucket straw bag measures 12½" x 12½" and has 6" leather double handles. Late 1940s – 1950s. Unmarked. $30.00 – 60.00.

Oh, the Bahamas — my favorite is truly Paradise Island; I just love Hurricane Hole! This is a tourist bag from the straw market. It measures 14½" wide and 12¾" high. Great detail! 1970s. $30.00 – 70.00.

Woven straw bag with a gold-tone barrel twist to close. Double handles in Lucite tortoiseshell color are 3½". The purse is lined in blue, gray, and white. A tag on the side pocket reads "SIMON MADE IN HONG KONG STYLED BY MISTER ERNEST." This bag measures 11" wide and 7½" high. 1940s – 1950s. $35.00 – 75.00.

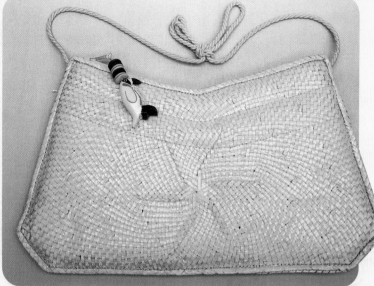

Yellow straw bag with a 20½" cord handle. A colored wooden parrot is on the zipper. The purse has a black linen lining with an open side pocket. "Hand made in the Philippines" is sewn on a white satin tag. This bag measures 13¾" wide and 7¾" high. 1980s. $30.00 – 75.00.

This tri-colored clutch measures 13½" wide and 9" high. A 20" twisted rope cord handle that lets this clutch become a shoulder bag is included. This purse has a red lining and a zippered pocket. A black tag reads "ANTON MADE IN ITALY." 1980s. $35.00 – 75.00.

The vinyl used for this bag is made to look like straw. The single handle is 5½" and is attached to a gold-tone frame that has a twist closure. This purse is lined in black vinyl. Unmarked. Measures 11" wide and 6¼" high. 1950s – 1960. $20.00 – 40.00.

Tasteful Tapestry

This bag is cream colored and has a border of black, and the same design is on both the front and the back. This purse has a gold-tone frame and a gold-tone single chain rope handle. It is lined in black satin and measures 9½" wide and 6" high. Unmarked, mid-1950s – early 1960s. $40.00 – 90.00.

This is a mid-1940s or early 1950s sleek design. A decorative gold-tone ring in the front attaches to the clasp. A frame of black vinyl has a matching handle attached. This bag measures 15" wide and 5¾" high and has a bone-colored vinyl lining and a single-side zippered pocket. Unmarked. I found a receipt that read "10/19" but did not have the year documented. The receipt also said, "Amt. sale $10.37 Penn Traffic dept. 60 Clerk 38." I left the receipt in the bag. $45.00 – 95.00.

Floral tapestry bag from the 1940s or the mid-1950s. This is unsigned and measures 12¾" wide and 8" high. A single black vinyl handle attaches to the gold-tone frame. $35.00 – 75.00.

This purse is lined in black satin. The front and back floral designs are done in muted greens, reds, and blues on a heavy black fabric. A black vinyl frame with a single handle attached is a nice example 1940s style. The top of this bag snaps to close. Excellent condition; looks like this purse was not carried. Unsigned. $40.00 – 90.00.

This should have been a tapestry! This bag has a detailed young loving couple on satin, a gold-tone frame, and a single chain for a handle. It measures 6¼" high and 8" wide and is signed "MADE IN ITALY" on a blue tag. Early 1940s – early 1950s. $45.00 – 105.00.

Swinging! The cloth cover of this photo album is taken from a feminine painting of a girl on a swing. This album was meant to be carried in your purse to show off your prized photos! If this were a tapestry, it would be outstanding! It measures 4" high and 3" wide. Unmarked. 1950s. $40.00 – 90.00.

"Saks 5th Ave Italy," 1930s. This billfold has a coin purse and two open side pockets. It is covered in fabric, with a beautiful painting of a lady sitting at her desk and looking at a book. Excellent detail. The back is black satin. This can be carried in your purse. It would make you want to own a tapestry! $45.00 – 95.00.

This purse has a tortoiseshell Bakelite frame on both sides, a matching 7¼" chain-link handle, and a floral tapestry of muted corals, lavenders, greens, and beiges. It has a satin lining in a butterscotch color. It has a zippered side pocket, and the zipper reads "EXCE." This bag measures 14" wide and 9" high. Early 1940s. $60.00 – 110.00.

Three for the price of one! Truly one of a kind! A clear plastic handle attaches to a gold-tone frame. The purse is lined with black nylon on one side and a carpet-like fabric on the other. Measures 9⅛" x 7½". Unsigned. 1940s. $60.00 – 110.00.

"KADIN MADE IN USA" is in black lettering on a white satin tag. This bag measures 11" wide and 7¼" high and is from the 1940s or early 1950s. It has double tapestry handles with vinyl sides. The snap is in the center; when closed, the top of the purse folds open to one side. A tortoiseshell frame in Bakelite is on one side only. The purse is lined in black satin and has a zippered side pocket. $50.00 – 100.00.

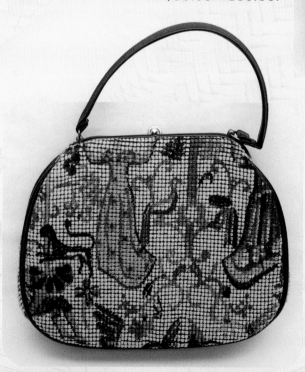

A single black vinyl handle attaches to this tapestry purse. There is great detail in the design. The purse is lined in black satin and has a zippered pocket with a black satin lining. A small gold-tone snap closes this bag, which measures 11" wide and 9" high. It is signed "EMPRESS BAGS MADE IN USA." 1940s. $50.00 – 105.00.

"EMPRESS BAGS MADE IN USA." 1940s. This is weighted and is lined in brown satin, and has a zippered pocket and an open inside pocket underneath. A single vinyl handle attaches to a brass clasp on each side of the frame. $50.00 – 100.00.

This purse has a fine needlepoint design of a floral bouquet bordered by flowers. It also has a gold-tone frame and a 5¾" gold rope handle. It measures 7⅛" x 5½" and is signed "MADE IN HONG KONG." 1930s. $105.00 – 145.00.

This cutch with a vanity and manicure set is lined in doeskin-colored suede. The manicure set is signed "MADE IN GERMANY" on the leather, and the fingernail file is signed "special triple cut" and "Germany." Original red paper tag bordered in black reads "Echt Stahl Germany" on one side; the other side has detailed crossed palm trees. This purse measures 7½" x 5½". 1940s – early 1950s. $85.00 – 125.00.

A unique square box bordered with a silver-tone frame; the top has a cut-out design. A clear Lucite handle gets lost on the silver frame. The silver border shows off the tapestry, a contrast to the handle. The purse is lined in black fabric with white embroidered snowflakes. The two sides are separated by lined cardboard. This handbag measures 8" wide and 7¼" high. Early 1950s. $125.00 – 145.00.

This bag has a gold stamp signed "DOVER MADE IN USA." It measures 14" wide and 10¾" high and has a tortoiseshell Lucite handle. A floral tapestry is on the front and the back. The purse is lined in black fabric. Two compartments are separated by a zippered inside. This bag closes with a silver twist snap set in black vinyl. 1940s – early 1950s. $60.00 – 100.00.

This unsigned purse is from the 1940s or the early 1950s. It measures 12½" wide and 10" high. A tortoiseshell Lucite handle is attached to a gold-tone frame. Sequins of many colors border the landscaped church scene. A red plastic chaton cut bead is at the top right, and a dark green bead is at the bottom left. The front and back have the same design; however, the back does not have the sequin border. This bag is lined in light gold satin. $75.00 – 135.00.

Fit for a queen! This 1940s bag is stamped "La FRANCE" in gold. There is beautiful depth to the floral design. The tapestry handle measures 6". A gold-tone crown clasp has topaz-colored pear and round rhinestones and gold-tone beads. This purse is lined in pea green satin, and has a zippered pocket and two open inside pockets on top of each other. The bag measures 12" wide and 7¾" high. $85.00 – 135.00.

The 1940s to the 1960s

This is a patent leather purse with a gold-tone buckle on the left and right of each side. A black cloth interior has a side zipper and a round gold tag that is signed "Kadin Made in USA." The purse measures 10" wide and 8½" high. It would be sharp to carry today to an evening winter wedding! 1950s. $45.00 – 75.00.

This 1950s brown vinyl bag is pretty for daytime wear and light outings. The frame is gold tone and has a snap closure. The bag has double handles. Its inside is lined, has a side zipper, and is stamped in gold; however, the stamping is worn and illegible. The purse is 10½" wide and 7" high. $35.00 – 65.00.

This black patent leather purse is signed "Garay" on a gold round cloth label on the inside zipper. It is lined in a heavier plastic and has tortoiseshell closures on a gold-tone frame. It measures 6¾" long and 9¼" wide. 1940s – early 1950s. I am sure the owner enjoyed carrying this dressy bag to all swanky social events. Today, I would carry this purse for dressing up or down. $40.00 – 80.00.

A single handle is attached to a gold frame with a snap closure. Plastic is over the satin fabric of this purse, which has the design of a basket and three pastel cut-out flowers. Seed pearls and gold roping are used throughout the design. A heavier gold cord is employed for the border. The bag has peach satin lining, and a large zipper pocket in vinyl over the fabric. It measures 12¼" wide and 8½" high and is signed "JR Florida, USA" in gold. 1950s. The stamping is starting to wear. This purse would still be great to carry today in the sunny South! $40.00 – 80.00.

Unmarked burgundy patent leather with clear plastic 6¾" chain double handles. The lining is ribbed satin in dark peach. The pocket is open on one side and zippered on the other. 1940s. $40.00 – 80.00.

This square is so stylish! This black patent leather purse has a gold-tone frame and a square closure. The handle is doubled and measures 4½" wide and 2¼" tall; the two halves of it are framed in gold-tone metal. The bag's black cloth lining is stamped "bobbie jerome" in gold. This purse looks like it was sold at a better department store. It measures 8" wide and 5½" high. Mid-1950s – early 1960s. $40.00 – 80.00.

This three-toned brown casual carry measures 13" wide and 6" high. The brown vinyl lining is stamped "Kismet Creations Made in USA." 1950s. A double handle in brown vinyl is attached to the gold-tone frame. $30.00 – 70.00.

This naturalizer handbag from the 1950s measures 10½" wide and 8½" high. It is of bone-colored vinyl and has gold rope trim at its midsection. The single handle is attached to the gold-tone frame, and the purse has a snap closure. It also has a ribbed dark brown satin lining. The inside side pocket holds the original square mirror. The original owner left a set of keys in the bag. $30.00 – 70.00.

This is a beautiful brown reptile bag. The dark brown satin lining is ribbed. There is a zippered side pocket on one side and an open pocket on the other. This bag measures 10" wide and 8½" high. Unsigned, 1960s. The original owner left a rope belt in the purse. I am sure any woman would have enjoyed sporting this purse. $60.00 – 110.00.

A single 10¾" tortoiseshell Bakelite chain on this black patent leather purse is attached to a tortoiseshell Bakelite frame. There is a snap closure to match. This bag measures 6½" high and 9¼" wide. Early 1950s. The ribbed black satin lining has a zippered side pocket. Paired with the right shoes, I am sure this would wow any girl! $90.00 – 130.00.

I would carry this for day or for evening. This is a soft vinyl purse from the 1950s, with double handles attached to the purse and a tortoiseshell Bakelite frame. The inside has a zippered pocket. The cream-colored plastic lining is stamped "JR U.S.A." in gold. The bag measures 7¾" high and 9½" wide. $75.00 – 105.00.

This is an unsigned purse, and I find that hard to imagine! This black leather 1950s bag sports a sleek frame and handle closure in tortoiseshell Bakelite. The lining is ribbed black satin, and the bag has a zippered side pocket. $90.00 – 130.00.

This flowered purse is from the 1940s or early 1950s. The single handle measures 5¼", and the bag itself measures 12" wide and 6" high. It is unmarked, made of suede fabric, and lined in black satin. On the left is a beaded flower that has a plastic bead in the center. On the right is a gold plastic flower that has small beads around a red plastic center. $45.00 – 95.00.

Splendidly scalloped tortoiseshell frame and handle in Bakelite. This black vinyl purse is lined in black ribbed satin and has a gold-tone frame. It measures 9¼" wide and 7¼" high. Unsigned, 1940s – early 1950s. $40.00 – 90.00.

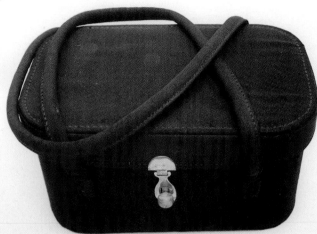

This eye-catching early 1960s pillbox-style purse is done in black ribbed fabric. It is lined in black satin and has an oval mirror on the inside of the lid. The double handles measure 6"; the purse is 7" wide and 4¼" high. I carried this to fundraisers in the early 1990s. $40.00 – 80.00.

Quality abounds in this 1940s, deep blue suede purse. It is stamped "blenen-davis" in gold on top of the inside pocket. It is lined in dark blue satin and has an open pocket lined in peach. The open pocket has two pockets: one is open and holds a blue satin case containing the original mirror for this beauty, and the opposite is zippered and holds the original coin bag, which has an attachable blue rope to help prevent loss. This purse measures 9½" wide and 7" tall and has a 4½" handle. $85.00 – 125.00.

This brown felt purse has a gold frame with black vinyl on top and a gold-tone closure in the center. It has a vanilla vinyl lining and a zippered pocket, and measures 12" wide and 7½" tall. Unmarked, 1940s. Carry to a card club or to go grocery shopping! $35.00 – 55.00.

"United States of America" says it all! How we love the red, white, and blue! This bag is great for the 4th of July or other summer holidays. The back is white only. The single handle measures 4¾", and the purse is 10⅛" wide and 7¼" high. The lining is black ribbed satin. An open pocket is stamped "non leather 3/26s 5186" in white. The gold-tone frame provides a nice finish. $40.00 – 80.00.

This mustard yellow purse is vinyl and has a gold frame and a clasp closure. The clasp has a yellow bar to match the bag. The lining is beige vinyl. A clear zipper is on the pocket. In the pocket is a receipt from Brody's in Indiana, Pennsylvania. The faded date reads "5-20-62." 12½" x 5½"; the single handle is 4". Early 1960s. $35.00 – 65.00.

This pink delight is a 1950s jewel. The single handle measures 4¾", and the purse is 10" x 10". The purse has a pink cloth lining, an open side, and a zipper pocket that has the original mirror and comb in a white paper bag. The bag is signed "Bobbi Jermone." A gold snap is used to close. $35.00 – 65.00.

This taupe clutch has a tortoiseshell handle. The lining is beige vinyl. A gold snap on the frame is used to close. 1950s. Unsigned. $28.00 – 48.00.

This green leather bag has a cream ribbed satin lining and a zippered side pocket. There is a gold stamp on the pocket that is fading and is very hard to read. The purse has a large gold twist snap closure. Two gold-tone links on each side suspend the 13⅛" x 10¼" frame from the handle. Late 1950s – early 1960s. $25.00 – 45.00.

This black patent leather bag is in great condition. It has a pretty silver satin lining that has black horizontal stripes and gold thread running through it. The bag is 15¼" x 14". 1950s – mid-1960s. $50.00 – 90.00.

This black patent leather purse has a silver twist closure on the front of the bag. The inside of the purse has a black plastic lining and a zippered pocket with a tag sewn on that reads "Virginia Slim Check Wear." The white paper tag reads "Made in China." This bag is 9¾" x 9". The strap measures 24½", and the handle is 3½". 1950s – mid-1960s. $25.00 – 45.00.

This black patent leather bag has a zippered center that opens to a two-sided pocket that has a center, zippered front pocket. The black plastic lining is simply gorgeous. This purse is 10⅛" x 6¼". The double straps measure 12". Unsigned, 1950s – mid-1960s. $30.00 – 50.00.

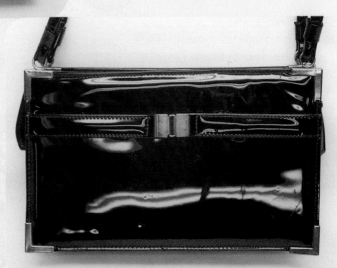

Miscellaneous

This pea green wooden purse has a gold velvet lining. The box has brass hinges and a white Lucite handle. There is a delicate floral design on the front and the top. The purse measures 9" x 4¾". Unmarked, dates from the 1960s. $90.00 – 140.00.

Enid Collins wooden box. There is a full mirror inside. Enid Collins designed bags for Neiman Marcus. Signed on the left front "Trees Kores R ec C." The three flowers are plastic and metal, and are a highly ornamental decoration for the purse. The center flower's top petal is damaged. This purse measures 8½" wide and 4½" long. 1960s. $90.00 – 150.00.

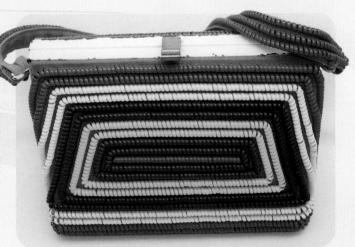

Can you hear me now? A colorful phone cord purse from the 1960s was originally offered in the Sears catalog. It has a black lining and an open side pocket. The frame is enameled white and shows some wear. This bag measures 8½" wide and 6¼" tall. Unsigned. $35.00 – 85.00.

This brown fabric purse has a cloth handle. A gold-tone frame accents the ribbed fabric. The center has a zippered pocket; the inside is quite stiff. Unmarked, measures 6½" x 6". 1950s. $30.00 – 60.00.

Black Lucite handles separate to open this beauty that is open in the center. A zippered pocket opens to reveal a smaller, open pocket. Hot flamingo pink felt lining is employed in this bag, which is marked "Jollies original" and measures 11" high and 10½" wide. This purse exemplifies the 1950s, with the front decorated in black and mother-of-pearl seed beads. Emerald green, crystal-shaped marquises in molded plastic make this bag the ultimate flamboyant accessory. The purse is slightly stained on the top right of the swan's tail. $55.00 – 125.00.

Bucket purse with a 5¾" handle. Green, pink, and aqua jewels and sequins are on the front of the cream-colored fabric, and a golden rope borders the three-dimensional design. The bag has wooden sides, an interior side zippered pocket, and an open pocket. 10" x 10". Unsigned. 1950s. $45.00 – 85.00.

This boxy blue vinyl purse with a pink and white stripe on the flap reminds me of someone so dainty! The lining is in royal blue satin. There is a mirror on the inside flap. The double handles measure 3¼", and the box is 8½" wide and 3¼" high. Unsigned. 1950s. $30.00 – 70.00.

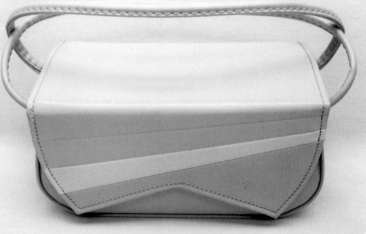

This bag measures 11" wide and 10½" high. The handle is 6½". The flap and bag are bordered in a gold-tone braided rope. The back design does not have the gold accents. The purse is lined in white satin and is all hand sewn. Above the open pocket is a hand sewn tag that reads "MADE IN JAPAN" in blue thread. 1950s. $50.00 – 90.00.

Remember the old party lines? This phone cord bag in three colors is lined in army green satin. It measures 7¾" wide and 4¼" high. Unsigned, 1960s. $20.00 – 40.00.

This early 1950s wooden box has such a fun design! The red bandana lining is appropriate. The two tortoiseshell Lucite handles are a sassy finish. This purse measures 7¼" high and 6¼" wide. Unsigned. Katie uses this for her nail polish kit! $45.00 – 85.00.

This wooden purse from the late 1950s is lined in a black felt. The off-white Lucite handle measures 4½" and is attached to the gold-tone hinged back. This handbag measures 4¾" high and 7¾" wide. $60.00 – 100.00.

Compacts & Accessories

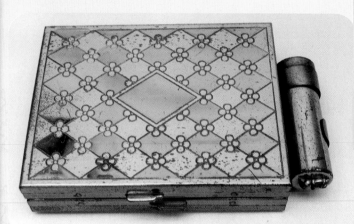

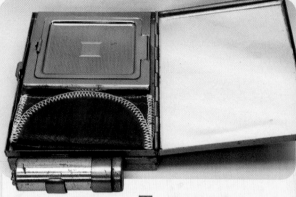

This is a two-way cigarette case with a mirror, comb, compact, and lipstick case (on the side). The lipstick case has an imitation ruby on the top to cap it off and make it look more finished. Both case and lipstick case are brushed gold and very weighty. 1950s. $100.00 – 130.00.

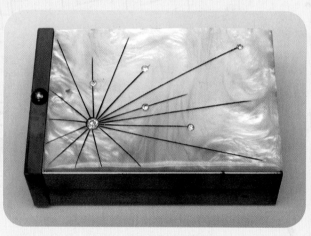

This is a classy mother-of-pearl cigarette case from the 1950s that is unmarked. The front has five small rhinestones shooting from a star, as rays, and one nice center rhinestone. This case measures 3½" x 2⅛". $60.00 – 100.00.

This cigarette case has a brushed gold-tone frame with small, off-white colored seed pearls. It measures 3¾" x 3". Unsigned. 1950s. $90.00 – 130.00.

A powerful pillbox from the 1950s, with a brushed gold back and a Lucite top. 2¼" x 2½". $50.00 – 70.00.

This gorgeous yellow wonder is a brushed goldenrod compact with an etched floral design and a full mirror inside. 2¼" x 3¼". 1950s. $55.00 – 75.00.

The inside of this compact and the powder puff's top are both signed "Harinet Hubbard AYER." There is a very intricate swirl design on the top. $55.00 – 85.00.

This 1950s compact is brushed silver, with gold bars and a gold border that is etched. It is stamped "USA" and "Front Golden Ann. 1905 – 1955 Rotary International." The silver backing has a golden border and golden center lines. The inside has a full-sized mirror with a powder puff. The puff's top reads "Zell 5th Avenue!" Excellent condition. $75.00 – 105.00.

This Art Deco compact is signed "Parenton" on the back. A full mirror completes the inside, and the powder puff is signed "Estee Lauder." A blue, gray, and white design on silver completes this masterpiece. 1940s, 3¾" diameter. $80.00 – 110.00.

This compact from the late 1940s has a black enameled top with gold-tone flowers. The back is done in gold, with a design of small diamonds separated by double gold-colored lines. This case has a full mirror. Unsigned, 3¾" round. $80.00 – 100.00.

Pampered peacocks! This cigarette case measures 3⅛" x 4¼". $70.00 – 90.00.

This pleasantly pink compact has blue and silver intersections on the front. A full mirror is inside. Unsigned. $80.00 – 100.00.

This 1960s tortoiseshell plastic powder puff case is from HB, Hazel Bishop Makeup. 2¼" diameter. $30.00 – 40.00.

This 2¾" diameter gold-tone compact from the early 1960s is unmarked. $30.00 – 50.00.

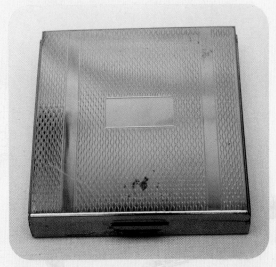

Raised letters read "Heart Thumpers." This is a mini photo album in which to put your sweetie's mug. The album has brushed gold backing. 1950s era. $30.00 – 50.00.

This compact is done in gold-tone and has a mirror inside. Very 1950s. The front center of this would be an ideal place for engraving a loved one's initials. $30.00 – 50.00.

This is a rather weighty silver compact with the original mirrors inside. "Silver plated by Pilcher" is inscribed, with black lettering, on the round silver tag. 1950s – early 1960s. $40.00 – 60.00.

Wind up the windmills and let the clouds roll. This compact has a back done in onyx. Unmarked, 1940s – early 1950s. $30.00 – 60.00.

This 1940s – mid-1950s silver-tone round compact measures 1¾" in diameter and has a ribbed design on the front. The back has three-dimensional circles. A place on the top front is ideal for initial inscription. $40.00 – 50.00.

This luminous lighter is from the 1940s or 1950s and measures 2¾". A unique tortoiseshell Lucite was used for it. The lighter comes with a black leather pouch. $30.00 – 50.00.

Twin tubes! These matching lipstick tubes from the 1970s would be ideal for best friends, sisters, or mother and daughter pairs. A fancy floral design is employed. 2¾". $12.00 – 24.00.

Fiesta! These immaculately kept tubes are Cover Girl from the late 1960s or the early 1970s. Silver confetti flecks are used. $12.00 – 20.00.

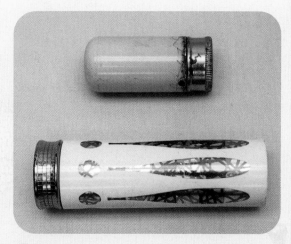

A lipstick holder (top) from the 1950s that is signed "Hong Kong" contains Coty 24 Brick Red. The holder has an etched floral design in gold on blue, with a white border. $20.00 – 30.00.

Perfumer (bottom) with a gold tag that reads "Avon," 3½". $12.00 – 18.00.

Cashmere bouquet (top) is stamped on the bottom "MADE FOR COLGATE, Jersey City, Made in the USA." 1950s – early 1960s, 1⅛". $13.00 – 23.00.

Lipstick (bottom) is signed "CG" on the top; however, the tag is worn away. 1970s. $15.00 – 25.00.

Signed "Schwartz Bros. Plastics, In Glendale, Calif. Des. Pat. Pen." The back of this is hinged to open. A holder can be found on the top of the inside, with a lid for a powder puff. This is baby blue like the Colorado sky, with a white flower on the top. 1950s. 4¼" diameter. $30.00 – 60.00.

This round sewing kit is from the 1940s or the 1950s, and is covered with leather and decorated with needlepoint. The center design is floralesque. $20.00 – 40.00.

Rocking red velvet stamped "Hand Warmer" with gold-tone lettering. Men, use when hunting; women, use when Christmas caroling. Marked "Made in Hong Kong." 1940s. $25.00 – 45.00.

The tag on this reads "BIG WHEEL 6476-10/9 2.48 Allspun Face Powder Naturelle Light Pinktone Cory Div Pfizer, NY. NY 10817. Compounded In USA." A white Max Factor powder puff is marked on the satin ribbon. Never used. $18.00 – 20.00.

My Favorite Three Gifts

This Coach bag is stamped inside. It says, "This is a Coach bag. It was hand crafted in the United States of completely natural glove tanned cowhide. The variations of grain are characteristics of natural full grain leather. No. B6C-9755." It measures 9½" wide and 6¼" high. The shoulder strap is optional. There is an open pocket on the inside and a pocket under the flap. The bag has a gold-tone twist closure. This was a Christmas gift to me from my best friend in the late 1990s.

Judith Leiber's bag is topped off with a gold-tone rose adorned in pavé crystals and with a center pearl. The clutch is lined in peach satin. Each side has an open pocket, with one holding the coin bag and the other holding a gold mirror. The original price tag in the bag reads "Neiman Marcus $990.00." The flannel bag that stores the clutch is signed "Judith Leiber" in white, and the tag inside says "MADE IN SPAIN." This purse measures 8¼" wide and 6⅛" long and includes a 20" gold-tone chain so it can be used as shoulder bag.

Cat napping! This precious Judith Leiber holds the original petite coin purse, comb, and mirror. The bow of pavé crystals makes one take notice even if he or she is a not a cat lover! The bag to hold accessories is stamped "Judith Leiber MADE IN ITALY." The bag to hold the purse is stamped "MADE IN SPAIN" inside. The lining of the cat is gold tone. This piece measures 6¼".

Each of these was given to me with warmth and sincerity, with each giver knowing I would love the gift. These three will go to Katie one day. They will always be my best and favorite purses. They are priceless.

Katie's Favorites

These are some of the purses Katie has used throughout the 19 years of her life. These three — the telephone purse, the solid and multicolor purse, and the Little Mermaid purse — are from her toddler years. No prices available.

She became trendy in her elementary school years, sporting shoulder denim and a drawstring crocheted lace. No prices available.

Her Coca-Cola purse was made of recycled Coke cans with writing in Thai. I bought this for her collection in Florida in 1998. No price available.

Red is her favorite color; this faux fur bag was made for Katie. No price available.

My dad bought the center straw bag for me at the straw market while on a family trip, when I was in eighth grade. The two in the front I bought for Katie while I was shopping in the same straw market years later. Katie and I have enjoyed every minute of being together while looking for her beloved purses. No prices available.

About the Author

Ronna Lee Aikins is the author of *Brilliant Rhinestones* and *Costume Jewelry 1900 – 1980.* She has been interviewed on national radio and has had articles about her books in magazines. Ronna and her daughter, Katie, have collected purses for the past 18 years. This book is based on their collections. Ronna also once owned a unique boutique that sold vintage purses and clothing. Ronna is involved with select antique shows and assists in antiques organizations. Ronna can be reached via e-mail at ronna@ronnas-antiques.com; Ronna's web site is www.ronnas-antiques.com. She resides in Blairsville, Pennsylvania.

Note from the Author

I hope that each collector who buys this book is delighted by the collection. The book covers a broad range of purses. If you like jewelry, you may enjoy my previous books. Please feel free to visit my website or contact me via email.

Values and prices reflected in this book are determined from what the purses are selling for in co-ops, antique stores, shows, flea markets, and auctions. Prices differ geographically. Also, the price is based on condition, quality, documentation, and designer.

Thank you for purchasing this book. If you have questions or comments, e-mail me at ronna@ronnas-antiques.com. I am looking forward to hearing from you!

Bibliography

Bell, C. Jeanenne Bell., G.G. *Answers to Questions about Old Jewelry*, 6th edition. Iola, WI: Krause Publications, 2003.

Dolan, Maryanne. *Vintage Clothing 1880 – 1960.* Florence, AL: Books Americana, 1987.

Hagerty, Barbara. *Handbags: A Peek Inside a Woman's Most Trusted Accessory.* Philadelphia, PA: Running Press Book Publishers, 2002.

Harris, Kristina. *Collector's Guide to Vintage Fashion Identification & Values.* Paducah, KY: Collector Books, 1999.

Holinger, Richard. *Antique Purses: A History ID & Value Guide.* Paducah, KY: Collector Books, 1987.

Huxford, Sharon and Bob Huxford, eds. *Schroeder's Antiques Price Guide.* Paducah, KY: Collector Books, 2002.

Johnson, Anna. *Handbags: The Power of the Purse.* New York, NY: Workman Publishing, 2002.

Marsh, Madeleine. *Miller's Collectibles Price Guide.* Heron Quay's, London: Octopus Publishing Group LTD, 1999.

Mason, Elizabeth. *Valuable Vintage.* New York, NY: Three Rivers Press, 2002.

Schwartz, Lynell. *Purse Masterpieces Identification & Value Guide.* Paducah, KY: Collector Books, 2004.

Smith, Pamela. *Official Price Guide To Vintage Fashion & Fabrics.* New York, NY: House of Collectibles, 2001.

Turudich, Daniela. *The Vintage Fashion Directory.* Long Beach, CA: Streamline Press, 2002.

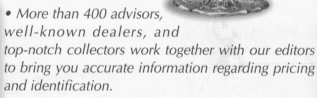